NIKKY'S NOTE

© 2024 Ginger Brown

All rights reserved.

No part of this publication may be reproduced, distributed, or transmitted in any form or by any means, including photocopying, recording, or other electronic or mechanical methods, without the prior written permission of the publisher, Parker Publisher and Author, Ginger Brown except in the case of brief quotations embodied in critical reviews and certain other non-commercial uses permitted by copyright law.

gingermbron311@yahoo.com

Dedicated to my beautiful daughter...Nikky.

Then, the Suicide teaches us that losing someone we love, as unbearable as it is, pales in comparison to the heavy burden of existence they carried all along...

Table Of Contents

Nikky's Note 1

Christy Ramsey 4

Preschool 7

French Immersion School 10

Playing Chess 17

Baseball 20

Golf 26

Moving To Our New House 27

How Nikky Met Evan 30

Kairi 34

The Sled Raft 38

Origami Flowers 42

Mistaken Song Lyrics 44

John Henry 47

Appreciating Camping 50

Graphic Design 52

Nikky's Hair 57

Her Love Of Reading 61

Nikky Breaks The News Of Her Sexual Orientation 63

Nikky And Evan Broke Up 65

My Goodbye 71

Losing Nikky 73

Birthday Parties	78
Finding The Note	82
Her Service	88
You Were Right	91
Evan And Kairi After Nikky	94
Surviving I'll Go First	98
Epilogue A Visit From Nikky	102
Her Tree Dedication	105

NIKKY'S NOTE

I had not found her note yet...

The police had just left. It was closing in on 4 AM. Sitting on the steps of our split foyer home in Greenbelt, my head leaning on the wall, I spoke to my daughter. "I love you Nikky, and I understand."

Hindsight isn't 20/20. In the existence in which we now live, there is no such thing as a 20/20 vision. We are like the old man with the thick horn-rimmed glasses, doing our best to make our way, all the while knowing there is much more to see. But we are not meant to see it, not yet anyway.

People with gifts like hers in everything they touch often seem to come with this sadness. It goes hand in hand with the most influential and beautiful of our world. It may be what makes them who they are. For her, though, the suffering became unbearable. She was so sensitive about others; animals, and the world. I wonder if she felt a responsibility to make everything ok. She sure seemed to try to do that for everyone she knew.

There was something exceptional about Nikky from the very beginning of her 21 years of life. She did everything early as if she were on fast forward, from smiling to laughing to talking and walking to seeming like a four-year-old at the age of two. The first time she laughed, she was only two months old, and it was at my expense.

She was sitting in her crib, holding on to the bars, watching me. I was trying to put a stack of clean baby clothes on a shelf, but the pile was too high. I thought I had it, but the entire stack toppled over and came raining down right on top of my head. To my shock, she didn't just laugh; she fell back laughing so loud and rolling from side to side! I couldn't understand how this little baby even knew that was funny! It's not like we could teach her that. In the days and years to follow, we would hear that lovely laugh over and over and, usually, at some silly mistake or accident. She always had the impish sense of humor of a male. One might argue that there isn't a difference in humor when it comes to gender, but if you were to look at the three stooges, for example, I would guess about 99% of males find it hilarious. Females, not so much.

I will always remember being asked to put 'Fantasia' on over and over, but she wouldn't watch it. She would paint. I didn't understand that it was classical music she was asking for until my 2-year-old was painting a child's rocking chair with flowers and a sky. She showed me a storm with dark clouds and grass blowing in the wind. "This is the part where the music becomes more dramatic." She explained as she pointed to the illustration. I then invested in classical CDs, which she had learned inside and out. We painted, drew, and made ornaments, and we did arts and crafts with classical music in the background daily.

The next year, we went to see 'The Nutcracker' at 'The Puppet Company Theater.' It was shown at Glen Echo Park, an affluent area just outside of Washington, DC. As the music started, Nikky, now 3 years old, happily exclaimed, "Tchaikovsky!!" She then surprised me by naming each of the ballet's arrangements. We watched, seated on the carpeted floor in the dark. Crowded around us were other children with their parents and nannies.

Nikky's Note

They all leaned in and listened while Nikky narrated. As each composition began, in a hushed voice, she would explain what each piece was about. One mother kept looking at me throughout it all until I finally explained. "Her interest in classical music started with Fantasia." "Oh," she said, "she's quite knowledgeable."

CHRISTY RAMSEY

Going back to work after having a baby sounds so simple. Take some time at home with the baby. Find daycare and go back to work, right? Well, for me, it was not so easy. It felt like betraying Nikky's trust. I first went back to work at Prince George's Community College as an interpreter for the hearing impaired. That was because they have evening and weekend classes, so I could work when Nikky's dad was home. Unfortunately, her first ear infection came on his watch. She couldn't drink her bottle because it hurt her ear. She was hungry, so she kept crying for the bottle and then crying from the pain. He was understandably extremely distraught but very relieved when I got home. I had done a lot of babysitting in my time, and I knew the signs of an ear infection. Those became chronic immediately. She would later become the youngest baby to have tubes put in. The tubes failed. She had chronic ear infections for her first 18 months. She then had her adenoids out and never had an ear infection again. When she got the ear infections, she'd spike temperatures, sometimes up to 104 degrees, and I'd have to give her a tepid bath to cool her. It always happened at night. She could not be sleep-trained because if she cried, it was usually a high fever, and she was back on antibiotics.

Even going out to dinner was really stressful for me. It was also stressful for the family member who would babysit, as well as for Nikky. I couldn't enjoy myself at all. I felt so worried the whole time. Nikky would cry the whole time we were gone. I honestly felt terrible leaving her. Then came

Nikky's Note

Christy Ramsey.

I would walk Nikky in her stroller/carriage across the street to the swings and then all over Greenbelt. Christy was 16. She lived in the court across the street. She always came right over with a big smile, wanting to see the baby. She would walk with us and chat happily. One afternoon, she asked, "Can I push the carriage?" I first looked at little Nikky's face and then at my hands, gripping the handle of the carriage tight. I looked up at this sweet 16-year-old's face. She had an expression of hope. Such an innocent thing to want to push the baby in the carriage. I thought, "I can trust this person." I peeled my hands off, and Christy took over. That was the beginning of a very important integral relationship that would go on through Nikky's young life.

Christy first became Nikky's babysitter. I could actually go out to dinner and a movie and come home, and everything was fine! Nikky would be sleeping peacefully. When I worked for an agency as a Nuclear Med. Tech. PRN at different hospitals, Christy became Nikky's daycare provider. One day, I realized I could work a whole day and know Christy would call if needed, and Nikky would not only be fine but happy. Finally, I did regular work, and it wasn't stressful. It was like having Mary Poppins right across the street.

One day, I noticed Christy had a little baby bump of her own. She hadn't told me, but we were so close, and me being me I just asked: "Christy, are you pregnant?" "Yes," she said, but she looked scared to tell me. "Well, why didn't you say so? You will be such a wonderful mother!" I said. "You really think so??" She asked with surprise in her voice and a relieved, happy look on her pretty face. "I absolutely KNOW so!" I said. Nikky later grew together with Christy's daughter, Katelyn. Christy treated them like sisters. At her young age, Christy was an amazingly awesome mom. She still is. She is also a very strong woman. I know Katelyn is, as well.

Years after Nikky died, Christy, Now Christy Ramsey Cupp, and I reconnected on Facebook. She and her husband made me a beautiful memory box. It has Nikky's face shellacked inside of the lid. It came with jewelry handmade by Christy and the most moving 'Thank you' card. The note in the card told me she had wanted to tell me for decades how important it was in her life that I had believed in her when she was young and scared, and no one else had. You just never know how much of an effect you can have on others by seeing who they are and what they are capable of and telling them when they need to hear it.

Nikky's Note

PRESCHOOL

It wasn't just art that Nikky loved. She loved reading and science and math, too. One day, my still 2-year-old saw 'The Magic School Bus.' She decided she wanted to go to school immediately. "When can I have a lunchbox and ride the bus to school?" She asked.

I had been a teacher's aide at a preschool called "Mom's Morning Out" when I was pregnant with her. It was for three to five-year-olds, but I knew she'd fit in. When We went to apply, the person at the desk who knew me and knew her age regretfully informed me that she was too young. Fortunately, the teacher saw us through the window and came into the office. "Of course, Nikky is welcome in my class!" Miss Gaye exclaimed happily. I didn't realize she thought Nikky was about 4 and that I had been pregnant with her younger sibling at the time when I worked with her. Nikky, mind you, was an only child. She repeatedly asked Nikky if she had a younger brother or sister. Nikky said no. Gaye then decided I must have lost the baby, and that is why Nikky never met him or her. Towards the end of her first year, the teacher told me that Nikky was ready for kindergarten. "The kids are learning the alphabet, but Nikky can already read and write," Gaye told me. "She is beginning to get depressed". It was the first time I had heard that word in connection with my daughter. Gaye had no idea this was a child who had just turned three, and I had no idea Gaye was unaware of her true age.

I approached Nikky with apprehension about her being 2 years younger than her classmates for her entire life. The social side of school would be so complicated and difficult. Not to worry, though, her response was, "I don't want to go to school with older kids. I want to go to school with kids my age, but I want to learn NEW things. I am sick of the letter 'J'." This was a dilemma. Speaking to another mom in my small town, I discovered French Immersion School. That would make even the alphabet new because it would be taught in French. The problem remained they didn't start until the age of 5. Nikky and I decided together that Nikky would continue preschool, and we added Ballet to keep her with kids her age. We added "big girl school" at home. She took this quite seriously. We would sit at the table, and we would roll through subjects. I was called 'Teacher'. I used home school books, and she was on a 4th-grade level in most subjects by the age of 5 when she was old enough for French immersion school. Spanish immersion was not available then, but she later picked that and Russian up, too.

When Nikky outgrew the preschool, thankfully, my long-time friend Alexa was working in the office. I went in searching for something new for Nikky. Alexa suggested Nikky join 'Creative Kids Camp'. My first thought when I heard the word "*camp*" was it was not for Nikky. I'd tried to get her to go. She couldn't understand why you'd sleep in a bag when there were perfectly good beds around. I even put up a tent in the yard like my parents used to do so we could sleep there. I dosed and woke up alone. She was inside in her bed. "OK," I thought. Maybe it's not for her. I didn't know yet, but later, she would learn to love camping. Thankfully, in Creative Kid's camp, there were no tents, no sleeping bags, and no nights without electricity. 'Creative Kids' was a day "camp" where you went to the community building and worked on plays. The plays were written by my friend who lived across the sidewalk from my parents, Chris Cherry. The kids would put a play on every 2 weeks. The kids would learn the lines and songs and the dances and help work on the costumes and the set. It was truly amazing. Nikky loved it. She lit up on stage! I'm a crybaby, and they would sing a song that got me every time. The songs were quite moving, and the kids of all ages were so talented. Chris worked with them, and they adored him.

Ginger Brown

FRENCH IMMERSION SCHOOL

Finally, it was time for kindergarten. My daughter would learn in French. There was a rule that for the first 2 years, the teacher could only speak French to the children. The reason being the students would have to learn French to 'survive.' I received a summons from the kindergarten teacher twice. Nikky had told me a few times that she was put in 'time out' and didn't know why. It didn't make sense to me. She was a very obedient child and very sensitive, so it was difficult to hear. Heartbreaking, actually. When I received the first summons, I was working at Mercy Hospital in Baltimore as a Nuclear Medicine Tech. Her school was in Bladensburg, Maryland. I came straight from work. Still wearing my scrubs, I quietly sat down where the teacher told me to and observed the class.

The class of 25 was sitting at 5 rectangular tables. The teacher explained as she dropped off a roll of paper towels and 5 bingo blotters at the end of the tables, each student should put 5 dots on one section of the paper towel. I am guessing the point being about working together and having someone at each table pass out the towel sections and blotters. The directions were in French. Nikky's table was the last to receive their supplies. Nikky and I had done multiple arts and crafts, but none of them were this simple. She reached out and quickly doled out the sections of paper towel as if she were dealing cards (which we played regularly at home). She then handed each of her 4 classmates a blotter. She blotted her section of paper towel with the 5 spots, and her group immediately followed suit. This all happened in under a minute. The teacher was helping a table nearby to choose someone to pass things out when Nikky tapped her and held up her towel section, saying, "We did cinq." (5) The teacher whispered in her ear, and Nikky returned to her table and spoke to the group. Their little hands went back to work with the blotters. I was a sign language interpreter and started teaching Nikky sign language as early as birth. I signed to her, asking, "What are you doing now?" "Teacher said do many, many dots," she signed back. Again, within minutes, Nikky got the teacher's attention and held up a section of paper towel completely covered in spots. The teacher instructed Nikky to sit at a separate desk over by the window away from the class but near me. Nikky pouted, skulked to the desk, and looked at me with a confused little face. The teacher waved me into the hallway.

"You just witnessed exactly what happens every day." The teacher explained in a hushed voice. Nikky finishes so fast and wants to do more, but I have 24 other students to work with. She thinks I am putting her in a 'time out' and I am not allowed to speak English to her to explain things. Please tell her when she is finished and others are still working, she can sit at the desk by the window and work on anything she likes. She can color or, paint, or read. She is not in time-out. She can bring supplies to work on while at that desk. There are markers and paper there that she can use."

I sent Nikky to school with a sketch pad. At the end of the year, it was full of happy works by her. Even at 5 years old, Nikky was extremely sensitive to the feelings of others. There was a girl in kindergarten who cried a lot and hated school. Nikky knocked herself out, trying to make that girl laugh. It was who she was and who she would always be right up until her last day in this world. So many friends were people she helped to brighten in dark times. Helping them helped her, too. She really felt the pain of others and would do anything to make it go away. She was a bright ray of sunshine, and she drew in every type of person. She was the least judgmental person I've ever known. She accepted all people. She found the good in them.

It reminds me of the scene in 'It's a Wonderful Life' when the suicidal George went to see Zuzu, who was sick in bed. "Fix it, Daddy," Zuzu said of her flower, which had lost some petals. Even in the mental distress George was feeling himself at that very moment, he didn't think for a minute to say, "I can't." George slid the petals in his pocket. "There." He handed the flower back to Zuzu. Zuzu was happy with the 'fixed' flower, and George was happy, too. That was Nikky's whole life. She was George. She had something else in common with George. She did not say this to hurt me, but being honest, she told me she wished she had never been born. She loved so many things in this world, but her mental pain outweighed that. She didn't wish to die. She just wished not to have existed in the first place.

The second summons came at Christmas time.

When I was in school, having a teacher call your parent was more often bad news than good, so of course, I was a little nervous when my presence was again requested by the teacher. I came after work, and the teacher waited until late in the evening to discuss what had happened that day. I entered the room and saw the walls covered in the artwork of a class of happy 5-year-olds. As I looked around, the teacher smiled and said, "Today, we painted Christmas scenes!" There were the classic skinny Santas by trees that they towered over with gift boxes almost the size of the trees. "Oh, they are so CUTE!" I said as I walked along, looking at the wall. "Yes," the teacher said, still smiling, but there was a little sarcasm in her voice as she waved her arm, palm up like a game show hostess to the last one. "And here's NIKKY'S!" There it was. I still have it. A perfect canvas covered in paint from corner to corner with four giant poinsettias in red and pink. The garden-green leaves are indicated with expert impressionist brush strokes. She stared at me, eyebrows up, waiting for my reaction. I could see by her expression that she wondered if I was aware of my daughter's unusual gift. "Oh..um,"... a little stammer, and then I looked at her and simply said, " Yes, I know." She giggled and said, "OK, just wanted to put that into perspective for ya!" She explained that Nikky had painted the poinsettias on standard kindergarten paper which is much too thin to stand up the paint over time. When the teacher saw Nikky's work, she asked where she had gotten that idea. "I saw them on some wrapping paper and thought they were pretty." Nikky had told her. The teacher then sacrificed one of her canvases from her limited supplies and asked Nikky if she could paint it again. The two paintings were completely identical stroke for stroke. I kept them both side by side for years until the one on the thin paper started cracking and falling apart. The canvas is still displayed in my house, calling me to remember what a special five-year-old Nikky Brown was.

In first grade, the teacher spoke with me to say that Nikky was being put into the TAG (Talented and Gifted) program. I was concerned she would be separated from her friends, or maybe some might feel they were not in her 'group.' I asked if we could do that without singling her out. The teacher agreed. I assumed Nikky didn't know she was in TAG, so I never mentioned it. Then, one day after school in 4th grade, she came home and said, "Oh my, Gosh, TAG gives too much homework! Leila doesn't have to do half of this! She's going to the movies, and I might not have time to go." By the way, Leila later became a veterinarian. She is a doctor now. The whole school was full of gifted kids. I said, "You knew you were in the TAG program?" She said," MOM, it says TAG on the board every year and there's my name on the list under it!" "Besides, how could I not know." "OH well, OK." It wasn't just the general courses she excelled at. There was a nationwide test for French-speaking ability. Nikky came in in the top 5% of the nation. I went to pick her up after the 'test,' which is an interview in French with people who have French as their primary language. The teacher, who was French and grew up in France, had watched. She was telling me Nikky had aced it. I guess I didn't act surprised, so she said. "You don't understand. She speaks with perfect diction, like a News anchor. I can't even do that!" Nikky never spoke French around me. I did hear her and her classmates speak it on occasion, but that was it.

Nikky would continue to impress her teachers every year. Not just because of her artistic ability but also because she had an interest in art history before she even started school. One day after school, Nikky, who was now in first grade, sadly told me, "I got yelled at in school today, and I don't know why." Knowing how extremely sensitive my daughter was and that she often thought people were yelling at her (myself included) when it was not the case at all, I immediately questioned whether it was a misunderstanding. "Who yelled at you?" I asked. "The teacher" This teacher, like most, adored Nikky. "Are you SURE she was yelling at you, sweetie?" "Yes," Nikky answered. And then she continued to explain to me "We were learning our vocabulary words (remember this is in French, but the student's primary language is English). She asked us if we knew what 'Talent' meant. I raised my hand and asked, 'Do you mean like Renoir?' And the teacher made a face like this..." Nikky now dropped her mouth wide open, eyebrows raised, and then she told me that the teacher yelled, "YOU KNOW RENOIR???" Nikky then added, "And Mom, then she kept looking at me like that!"

I realized it was probably even more surprising to a teacher from France. Later that year, the children were given an assignment to make a comic strip of a person in history doing something they admired. Already somewhat of a perfectionist, Nikky's was amazing. It was a timeline of Renoir's life. It went right through his painting and sculpting with crippling arthritis. She drew him painting as a young man. Then painting with his brushes strapped to his crippled hands. She drew him sculpting when painting became impossible. She drew him directing young sculptors from his wheelchair at the end. I must admit, I chuckled as my 6-year-old left for school with her comic strip that told more about Renoir than most adults would ever know.

When Nikky was a tot, we played the arcade game where you shoot baskets as fast as you can. My sister had played basketball for Eleanor Roosevelt High School, and thankfully, she had taken the time to at least teach me to shoot. We were in a child's game arcade at the mall. Nikky, the tiny tot, was standing on the ledge of the game with me holding her in place shooting, and she was killing it. A little boy about 7 stood and watched her in disbelief. When we finished the game, he yelled, "WOW! Larry BIRD!!" I called her 'Nikky Bird' for years after that. So, I had an idea that, unlike me, Nikky may be pretty good at sports. When she was five, we started playing "Around the World" on the basketball court behind our house. We'd also just take turns shooting. Now, this little girl could just stand at the foul line and shoot basket after basket. I told the doctor I worked with At Mercy, whose wife was a Basketball Coach at Seton High. Cathy told him to tell me to get her into Basketball camp immediately. That it wasn't too early, I discussed this with my very mature 5-year-old. She wanted to think about it. She then went to a Mystics game with her after-school group. She came home and informed me that "Those girls were ALL OVER each other. I am not playing a game like that!"

Nikky's Note

PLAYING CHESS

She was competitive at board games, but it worked out because she definitely won much more than she lost. I had a crystal chess set that intrigued her. She had asked me multiple times to teach her to play. I had played in tournaments as a 7 and 8-year-old, and I knew you had to do a lot of losing to learn that game. I did not share the competitive spirit Nikky possessed. In fact, I was surprised any time I won anything. A neighbor's grandfather was my chess coach. He lived down the sidewalk, so I'd go over and learn. We spent a LOT of hours, and he taught me exactly how to react to any combination of moves. It was memorization. Most kids that age would not sit to learn this game, but Mr. Grob had a bowl of toffees and sometimes tea served in pretty flowered cups with saucers, so I was all in. My siblings played too, but they got bored and dropped out. I sucked at first, but I kept coming back. Finally, after much coaching, I got to the point where I was a formidable player, however, I did not yet realize that. I then played in a tournament. I had expected to play other kids who had been coached. They were not. They had no chance against me as they should not have been expected to. I thought the first one just was nervous. When it kept happening over and over that I'd beat them in a few moves, I actually felt bad. They were cheated. In a way, so was I because I thought I'd play kids who'd worked at learning the game like I had. The kids were not at all upset, though. I kept winning and watching the players I had beaten skip happily off literally to a chocolate fountain, among other opulent amenities. I won the tournament. That was enough of that game for me. I then stopped playing in my mind for good. I got a trophy, but I didn't even show it to anyone, nor did I keep it, and I kept EVERYTHING. I did keep the crystal chess set, though. It was so pretty. I just wanted to look at it, not play the game.

I didn't want Nikky to dive into this game, so I always found a way to put off teaching her. I have to admit I didn't look forward to teaching her, but I knew the day would come eventually. I knew that once introduced to this game, she'd obsessively keep at it until she conquered it. In her case, not for tea and toffees.

One day, Nikky came home and said, "I'm in the Chess Club at school." I was worried, but I shouldn't have been. Nikky did not need the coach that I had. She learned how the pieces moved and the rules of the game, and I don't know how, but she just kept winning right from the start. The school had her play in older grades, but again, she just won and won. Finally, she lost to her older cousin. I expected her to sulk and want to keep trying to beat Jamie, but again, I was wrong about that, too. She told me: "I'm happy if I had to lose, it meant my cousin, Jamie, got to win. He was so happy." Then she asked if we could play.

I thought back to when I was 14. That had been the last time I'd played. I had gone with a group of School friends to visit a classmate, named Mary Millhollan, who lived in Boxwood. We were there to discuss something important, but I don't remember what. Whatever the subject was bored me. Probably homework. I drifted around, and then I saw a game on the coffee

Nikky's Note

table. It had images of chess pieces on it. I picked it up and found myself playing a game against a computer. I beat it in minutes. It made an extremely loud noise when I won, which startled me. Everyone in the room looked at me. Mary asked, "ARE YOU KIDDING ME??? Did you just beat that game??" "How did you DO that?" She put her hand out and demanded no one else touch the game. I gave it to her, and she put it up on a shelf. "My brother, Tim, is going to FREAK out. He has been trying to beat this game for a year!" I had not even thought I'd remember how to play, but I guess the coaching stayed somewhere in the recesses of my brain.

It was a dilemma. I didn't want to let her win, and I didn't want to beat her. I again didn't even think I'd remember how to play, but I was worried, so I said, "Nikky, I won't let you win. If you win, it's because you beat me when I was really trying." It was a long game. She didn't make it easy, but in the end, I won. I explained the coaching I went through and that I could not have won without it. That satisfied her, and we never played together again. She was on to sports next.

BASEBALL

Nikky decided to play baseball like her cousins. Her cousins were both males. Nikky had not noticed that girls generally don't play on the same teams as boys. She had me sign her up for little league. To be honest, I figured she'd look around and see she was the only girl and lose interest. NOPE. She took her responsibility as a team player extremely seriously from the first practice until she was too old to play any longer. She never missed a practice, never mind a game. We actually had to schedule vacations around baseball because she didn't want to disappoint the team. Unlike the way boys treated girls when I was young, the boys on her team treated her with the utmost respect from the start, as did her coaches. Her teammates' parents loved Nikky too. It felt like everyone there was on her side and wanted to see her succeed. Even the parents and players on other teams seemed to be on her side. I'm so glad she wanted to play so I could see and feel that. The team was the Greenbelt Giants. Her coach, Rich Wilson, was in his last year of coaching because his son was in his last year of playing. I'd ask Nikky if she had fun every day after practice or a game. No matter what, every time, the answer was a resounding YES! I was always there, as was her dad, my ex-husband. I looked forward to hearing her account of the game or practice. She'd tell me funny things that happened in the dugout. We normally played at McDonald's field, but sometimes we played at Northway fields. The last game of her first season was there. It was also going to be the last game for the beloved Coach Rich. After the game, Nikky climbed into my CRV. Coach

Rich was talking to some parents. No doubt they were saying sad goodbyes along with extending appreciation. "So, do you want to play next year?" I asked as I started towards the long dirt road path out of the fields. "Yes, I do," she said with sweat and dirt and a smile on her face. "OK, I said, but it will not be Coach Rich; it will be a new coach." Nikky's next words said it all: "Oh, then no." I knew he was important to her, and she was to him, but I didn't realize how much until that moment. I made a fast U-turn, kicking up a cloud of dirt and rushing to get back to Coach Rich before he left. I got out of the car and walked up to him. I told him what Nikky had just said. He smiled and said, "Tell Nikky I'll be there." He stayed on right through her last year in little league. He also threw her a goodbye party at his house. It was near a swimming park, where we all went and then back to his house for a cookout. He gave Nikky her jersey, which was signed by the team and coaches and framed.

Like everything she did, Nikky got to be quite a ball player. She could do it all. She was a great hitter; in fact, she was one of the few players who could hit it out of the park. The first time she would step up to bat against a new coach on another team, I'd hear the coaches yelling: "MOVE IN! MOVE IN! MOVE IN!" The second time she'd come up to bat, I'd hear the same coaches yelling: "MOVE OUT! MOVE OUT! MOVE OUT!" She caught everything that came her way, too. She was usually on first base. The instant the ball hit her glove, she'd send it where it needed to go next to get another player out. She had excellent aim, so the other player only needed to hold his glove up, and the ball was there. The players on other teams tried not to hit it towards first base because that'd likely be 2 outs. She pitched once and got the first three players up to bat out immediately, but she hated the pressure. In fact, she sat next to me and cried for a minute afterward. And we all know there's no cryin' in baseball, so she only did it once. By that time, Coach Rich was the manager, and Mike Lanier, who was the homicide detective for Greenbelt Police, was the coach. They both were kind enough to see how it affected her and not press her even though she would have been an ace in the hole. I really appreciated that so much. In retrospect, maybe they had an idea about how sensitive she was.

Each year, she also played on a fall team with older kids. The last year, lots of them were over 6 feet tall. She and a boy who stood 6'3" were the only two kids who hit it out of the park that season. This was not with her beloved Mike and Rich anymore. This was a regulation-sized park. Again, the boys accepted her immediately. One day, I was holding our tiny black and white Chihuahua, 'Oreo, ' and standing behind our home plate. The game was nearing an end with two outs. A teammate was at bat, and Nikky was on deck warming up. She was taller than me now. I'm 5'4" and she was 5'6". She would later grow 2 more inches. Her long blond ponytail stuck out of her ball cap. She expertly swung again and again. Two coaches of the team that would play next walked up and stood by me. The coach, around my age, was immediately annoyed to see a female playing. "Get a load of THIS," he grumbled. The other coach agreed. They could not possibly know who I was and actually looked at me, expecting ME to agree with THEM. I kept my face as straight as I could, while in my head, I thought, "OH YES, this is going to be really fun." The other coach listened as he grumbled on: "I can't believe it's come to this!" The teammate thankfully got a hit and he made it to second base. At that very moment, one of their players walked up, and Nikky stepped up to bat. I held my breath. CRACK went her bat and out... of... the....... PARK went that ball!!! "HOLY COW, DID YOU SEE THAT??" Screamed their player, standing with the three of us and pointing to Nikky, gently jogging around the bases. The other players were arriving now. "See that blond ponytail??" He asked each player, "She CRUSHED IT!" "She whacked that ball RIGHT OUT OF THE PARK! First pitch!!" He yelled to Nikky as she jogged to home plate. Nikky had a shy chuckle at his excitement. The coaches stared, frozen. The game wrapped up. Then the boy petted Oreo and continued reliving the hit to each kid as they arrived, calling Nikky the blond ponytail over and over. Just as Nikky headed our way, I said loudly, "and guess what?" to the boy. "This is the blond ponytail's dog you are petting right now." Both coaches jumped a little and stared as Nikky was approaching fast, just feet away now. "YEP!" I said to the coaches, "That's my daughter!" with a proud kind of 'in your face' smile. Nikky arrived to be JOYOUSLY congratulated by the boy. It felt like a scene from a movie, and I thoroughly enjoyed every minute of it! On the way home, I was telling Nikky about the boy's excitement. I didn't tell her about the coaches. That would have needlessly injured her. She told me about the high-fives in the dugout. I happily retold the incident countless times to anyone who would listen.

After Little League and the Fall Team, there were no Leagues for Nikky to move on to in Greenbelt. There was a softball for girls her age, but she said the ball moves too slowly, and it throws her off. She had a time when she had no team to play on, and she really missed Baseball. Then, 9th grade came around, and Nikky moved from French Immersion School at Robert

Goddard to Eleanor Roosevelt. One of the coaches had come and seen her playing Little League, and he was waiting for Nikky to come to ERHS. Now, Roosevelt is a very competitive school when it comes to sports, actually, when it comes to everything. It's a magnet school and has an amazing reputation, which is well deserved.

    I had dropped her off for tryouts and was dismissed by the coaches, as were all of the parents. Apparently, no helicopter moms are allowed around there! It was an awkward amount of time, so I picked up some breakfast from McDonald's. Fast food was unusual for us, so it was a special treat. I came back to pick her up in my car, filled with the lovely smell of egg and cheese biscuits and hash browns. She climbed in and said, "I'm on the team." She was already selected to play, actually the very first pick! She did not seem as happy about it as I'd expected. "You know ALREADY??" I asked. "They still have 2 more days of tryouts!" "Yeah, they said, ' Nikky, You're on the team. The rest of you look for your name on the board in the office later this week.' She said, still not sounding thrilled. "WOW, that's awesome!" I said. "I told you, you are an exceptional player!" Then, carefully, I asked, "Are you looking forward to playing again?" "Well," She said sadly, "The coach was really mean to some of the kids trying out." Nikky was a very caring and sensitive person, and seeing people being mistreated really hurt her. "Oh," I said, feeling her sadness. "Well, if this isn't fun for you, Sweetie, don't do it, but decide soon because once you are on the team, I know you, and you'll feel too bad to quit."

    I never played sports in High school. I was more of an aerobics workout fan. I loved running but didn't do it competitively. I didn't realize Nikky

Nikky's Note

could skip JV and get put directly on Varsity in 9th grade. When I told my long-time friend and now coworker, Doug Tull, that this had happened, he became concerned and had his daughter's friend speak to me about the varsity coach at ERHS. He was flat-out abusive to the girls.

On Nikky's first day on the team, a mom was minutes late in dropping off her daughter. The coach punished the girl, making her run around the field multiple times. The field was miles around. It was extremely hot out. The girl got sick. Nikky quit. It sounds weird, but I was actually relieved when she quit. Having heard a lot about that one coach, I knew his abuses would haunt Nikky even if it wasn't happening to her. Also, I am not a violent person, but I kept having this scene play out in my head where he abused a player, and I jumped over the fence to smack him. That probably wouldn't go over very well, so we avoided all of that.

Thankfully, Brooke Bailey's dad, a good friend, was playing on an adult team of NASA employees. He invited Nikky, and she played. I asked if they were more serious since they were adults. She laughed and said, "NO! They drink beer while we play!" We both laughed, and I knew it was perfect for her.

GOLF

Next, Nikky tried golf. Again, her cousins were attending a summer golf camp near Glen Dale. Nikky Joined. Can you guess how she did by now? She came home at the end with a long check list, a sort of report card from the camp. She aced every single thing on it. At the bottom, there was a note for her parents. It suggested we allow Nikky to start training to play pro golf. I still think of that when I watch the teenage females play. Her cousins really wanted to see her go pro, but she did not feel passionate about it and only wanted to play for fun. She had her own clubs and played with her dad from time to time. I didn't want to play.

Again, me and sportsball are a no. When her dad and I had lived in Florida for a couple of years, at the beginning of our marriage, he had talked me into trying it. I watched a video, and it turned out I could hit straight but not far. There was a short course in West Palm Beach where I played 18 holes with Charlie and his golf buddies. I could get on the green in 2 short shots and was good at putting. Charlie had wanted me to keep playing, but to me, it wasn't really that fun. It wasn't natural, so I had to keep telling myself what to do head to foot over and over. I couldn't just go up and hit the ball naturally. So, I understood Nikky's lack of passion for the sport.

That was it for Nikky's sports, but she always stayed busy with arts and crafts and work.

Nikky's Note

MOVING TO OUR NEW HOUSE

When Nikky was 12, I decided we needed more room so that she could have friends over, and I would not be right on top of them. I started searching for our next home. I looked around in nearby towns, but the perfect home turned out to be right here in Greenbelt. The house had a full living room in the basement with a fireplace, 2 rooms, and a bath down there too. The kids kind of had their own space, but I was right upstairs. It became one of two places the kids liked to gather. Our house, or Brooke Bailey's house, was where they were comfortable. I also really liked and trusted Brooke's parents so I was happy with that arrangement too. It was fun being allowed to know her friends. Nikky shared everything with me, but she normally didn't want me in the mix when they were over, which is understandable. Seeing how sweet this young group of humans was was so inspirational. A favorite game was called Dance Dance Revolution (DDR). Once in a while they'd invite me to play too. They were so kind to this old mom who couldn't do anything near what they could. I had a song that I always messed up on the same little riff of steps. Brooke was sitting in the primo seat, which was a giant cushy chez next to the dance pads right in front of the TV. You could watch everything. I messed up my riff, and the next time it came up, Brooke said, "DUT DUT DUU" in time with the steps and for the first time, I got through it. Then she said it every time it came up again, and I got through the whole song! It was so kind of her. I never messed that song up again because I'd think "DutDutDuu" every time I got to that part.

I also found hearing her friends' observations about me funny and eye-opening at times. For example, one night, they took a video of everyone playing DDR. It was one of the rare times I was allowed to play, too. I usually played when they weren't there because it was fun and great exercise. I could never play anywhere near as well as they could. I didn't even aspire to. Later, they laughed while watching the video and showed it to me. I was not aware until then that I held my arms in front of my waist, wrists, and hands bent down, and I jumped the whole time. "Mom, look how you jump!" Nikky said, showing me the video...."Oh my God!" I said, laughing. "I didn't know I did that! I look like a kangaroo!" After that, I always thought of it when I played, but it was just natural; I couldn't stop doing it.

There were really nice things about our house. We had vinyl flooring in the kitchen that was pretty, but I hated that I could never get a thin line where the floor met the baseboard clean. I couldn't reach it and scrub. I tried everything. One day, I was using a spinny electric toothbrush, and it suddenly occurred to me that I should try it. Worked like a charm! Getting rid of that line was quite satisfying, but with such a tiny instrument, it took a long time. I worked on it on weekends a lot. I'd always say out loud how great it worked as I did it.

One Saturday, Brooke came to the glass door while I was working on the floor, and I waved her in. I continued toothbrushing the floor. She stood there watching me for a few minutes, and I told her how well the tiny buffer worked. As she went down the steps, I heard her call out, "Nikky, I'm concerned about your mother!" I heard Nikky's distant voice ask, "Why? What is she doing?" "She's cleaning the kitchen floor with a toothbrush!" Brooke said. "Oh, yeah," Nikky said. "She loves to do that." Brooke's now distant voice said," Ohkayyy??" And they moved onto other things. I then realized it was a bit of an obsession. But I continued on, happily cleaning the stubborn line.

Something I love to do, which my Facebook friends kindly put up with, is to post cell phone pics of the Christmas tree ornaments up really close and at funny angles. I was working on my Christmas photo art, and the tree was in the basement living room that year. Nikky's boyfriend, Evan, came in, "Hello!" He called in the foyer. "HI, Evan!" I called back. He came down the steps. Like Brooke, he paused a while, then walked down the hall. I heard him say, "Nikky, your mom is weird; she's lying under the Christmas tree texting!" Now, Nikky totally knew what I was doing, but instead of explaining, she just laughed really hard and let Evan continue to think that! I decided to let him think it too. Nikky knew I wouldn't mind because whenever people said I was weird, I'd say, "Thank you." and she'd laugh.

HOW NIKKY MET EVAN

Nikky and her friends would go ice skating regularly. Nikky and I had gone since she was little. We had also roller-bladed. One night, Evan and a group of friends were there. The two groups became friends. When we had DDR nights, the new group now joined. Nikky actually briefly dated a friend of Evan's. He reminded me of a surfer dude combined with a hippy. His dad was a tattoo artist. His Dad's work interested Nikky. She actually designed tattoos later while in college. She worked at Starbucks then, and the police would stay there when they were closing to keep them safe. Nikky designed tattoos that some of the Greenbelt police now have.

Nikky's Note

I normally attended a Society of Nuclear Medicine meeting in Ocean City in April every other year to get my CEUs (Continuing Education Units) for my license and registration. I was there when my ex-husband, Nikky's dad, called me. "Hey, what's up?" I asked, "Umm... I don't want to break any rules here. Is Evan allowed to visit Nikky at your house?" He asked, "She wants me to pick him up." "Oh, yes," I said. "Evan is really nice. He's in her group of friends. It's fine", I said.

A few hours later came a life-changing call from Nikky. "Mom, can I go to the movies with Evan?" Nikky was 14. I was very particular about Nikky going out at night. "Nikky, you know I'm gonna say no," I said. "It's late." "PLEASE!" She begged. "Well, who would be driving?" I asked. "His Sister." I hadn't met Shakira yet. If I had, I would have immediately said yes. I had to know people before they drove my daughter around at night. "Nikky, I'm so far away. I'd be worried." I said. She then said, "Hold on," and walked out of earshot of Evan. "Mom, I think I like Evan.", She said in a hushed voice. "What makes you think so?" I asked. " We just sat here talking for 3 hours and I forgot to give him anything to drink, never mind eat." Now I laughed. "That's a pretty good sign that you like him!" I said. I was happy for her. "Mom, please let me go to the movie. You can talk to Shakira; She's really nice." She said. And that was the beginning. April 13th became Nikky and Evan's anniversary for the next 7 years.

I have to say they were about as perfect as a couple can get. They were both always doing something special and romantic for each other. When their first Christmas was approaching, they decided not to spend lots of money but to make their gifts by hand. Nikky's favorite colors were red and black. She now stood 5'8". She had a hard time finding things long enough for her height. She really wanted a scarf that would hang past her knees. She also needed a purse, but none of the ones we looked at were quite Nikky. Some are too formal, and others are too old-fashioned. Evan learned to crochet for Nikky that year. He made her the most perfect red and black purse with a super long strap, which she carried for the next 6 years. He also made her a really long red and black scarf which hung to the middle of her shins. She wore it every year. For Evan, Nikky made the first in a series of books illustrating their relationship. The books grew in dimension and complexity every year. The first was a romantic picture book. The second is a pop-up. Each year, the books have become more and more amazing. The final one was a masterpiece. It had pages made of triangular cardboard canvases that folded into a pyramid. The beginning of the story was on the outermost pages, illustrated with black and white photos and paintings of her and Evan. (She had taken photography at ER, and of course she was excellent.) The walls of the pyramid unfolded to reveal more paintings and photos on the inside, and more walls were within like wooden Russian dolls. It unfolded and unfolded, staying connected at the bottom by a square base. In the center was a 3-D sculpture of a black and red heart. Seriously, I think they topped 'The gift of the Magi'. They would continue learning new skills and creating more gifts for each other throughout the rest of their relationship. Nikky later also learned to crochet and made me hats and scarves that I, of course, still treasure.

Then came the year that Nikky asked for a Sewing machine as her main Christmas gift. It had specific capabilities. Her grandmother on her dad's side was no longer with us, but she had been an excellent seamstress. I'd say Nikky inherited the skill from Gem because I have absolutely no idea how to sew. She did amazing things for Evan and also made herself the cutest Nikky-style skirts that fit her height the way she wanted them to. Evan had fun with it, too. He made Nikky a thermal lunch bag on the machine, and he made a thermal handle cover for my cast iron frying pan, among so many other things.

KAIRI

Nikky's Note

Nikky had wanted a dog since she was little. She was convinced that a dog would help with her depression and anxiety. The problem was she was still at her dad's every other week then, and I was working at Mercy Hospital in Baltimore. We worked ten-hour days, and it was an hour's drive so I was gone too long. When I finally left Mercy for an office job, we got Oreo. Nikky picked Oreo from a pet store. She was still playing Little League Baseball, and Oreo came to every game and every practice. She was a tiny black and white Chihuahua. The coaches named her 'Rat Dog.' Nikky loved Oreo, but she later decided that she really wanted a bigger dog. Also, like a lot of Chihuahuas, Oreo was kind of a one-person dog. Oreo took to me. She'd only sleep with me. She was always in my lap. Nikky kept asking for a bigger dog that would be more hers. I told Nikky she would have to be responsible for the new dog. She would take the dog to the vet and on walks and feed the dog. In order to take the dog to the vet, she would have to have a driver's license.

Nikky waited to be old enough to drive and got a job immediately. All was inspired by the dog she was dreaming of getting. By this time, she was with Evan. Nikky researched dogs very thoroughly and decided on either a Britney spaniel or a Springer. Britneys were really hard to find, but she found a breeder who bred Springers. She waited for her new pup, and one day, a fat, furry little butterball came home with Nikky. Nikky loved the game 'Kingdom Hearts' and named Kairi after a princess in the game.

Kairi was a hilarious handful as a puppy. I've had dogs before, but never one that chewed things like this one. I decided to unapologetically wear my shoes with puppy tooth prints in them because she got them all. I had them on a shoe stand, but that did not stop the determined little pup. That seems par for the course, but one day, I went to get my glasses from the coffee table (mistake; she could reach everything on it), and she had chewed them into a gnarled mess. I learned to keep the new glasses in my purse at all times and way up high where she couldn't get it. One day, I was wrapping Christmas presents on the couch. Nikky wasn't home, which meant Kairi, who was a taller, gangly pup now, sat close to me. I was her third choice after Nik and Evan. I heard a loud crunch crunch of puppy teeth. "Oh no! What has she gotten now?" But the object was gone so fast. I couldn't figure out what she'd eaten. I went back to wrapping. I couldn't find the Scotch tape. It was JUST right here. Where... Ohhhhhnooooooo! It was the tape, alright.

Right then, Nikky came in. "I think we need to take Kairi to the vet!" I said in a panic. But Nikky would not believe it. She said there was no way she ate a whole tape dispenser that fast. It must be there somewhere. But it wasn't. I was so scared because Nikky immediately took Kairi to her dad's for a visit. I kept thinking the sharp plastic would tear her intestines up. Not to worry, because instead, her stomach melted the plastic. For the next few days, her poop sparkled in the sun with the melted plastic in it. I had to laugh at the sparkling poop! Hoping to give her something other than our things to chew, Nikky crocheted her a toy. It was really thick yarn crocheted tightly with a squeaky inside. It seemed like Kairi knew this toy was special because she took it with her everywhere, and she did not tear it up as we knew she could.

Nikky's Note

Nikky took her responsibility to care for Kairi quite seriously. She tried never to ask for my help. Unlike Oreo, Kairi knew full well she was Nikky's dog. She also knew Evan would watch over her, too. She was my "grand-dog," and of course, later became my baby. Nikky and I would walk our dogs together, which was very sweet for me because, at that age, even though we lived together and Nikky shared her day with me, a lot of things she did didn't involve 'mom,' which is as it should be. So, the walks were a thing we shared that meant a lot to me. We talked about everything on those walks.

Nikky and I both were interested in stars and planets. I have glasses for distance, but I only wear them while driving. We were walking our dogs together one evening, and it was really clear out. I looked up and saw the brightest star. It had to be a planet! I knew it wasn't Venus, though. Venus is normally the brightest in the night sky. "Nikky, look! What planet do you think that one is?" I asked with excitement. "MOMMM!!" Nikky said in a humorous voice, like Jimmy Fallon imitating a teenage girl," Put your GLASSES on! That's an AEROPLANE!" I stopped walking to see the planet moving through the sky. We both laughed so hard we had tears in our eyes. Our walk was 2 miles and we both kept thinking about it again and laughing uncontrollably again. After that, any time I saw a plane at night and Nikky was with me, I'd ask her what planet it was. It was our running joke. I think of that often when I walk Kairi at night, and I see an airplane. It still cracks me up.

THE SLED RAFT

When Nikky was younger, we had actual toy stores everywhere. You could go inside and see a huge room filled with aisle after aisle of toys, big and small, of all types. I loved feeling the wonder of a kid walking in, and I loved imagining how happy Nikky would be with this toy or that one. When she was 4 years old, I bought us what I call Sled-Rafts. There were the tubes like you use in a snow or water park, and there was one that was shaped like a full-length inflatable wide raft that two could sit on. It had handles to hold onto and rubber runners on the bottom. It was made of material similar to those yellow and black inflatable two-man row boats. You could lay on it on your belly and hang on and go down the steepest hills with the cushion under you, absorbing the bumps. I still had some kid in me, and I would laugh my butt off going down hills when it snowed. Nikky and I used them year after year.

Sledding was a huge part of winter for me and Nikky. There was a wonderful hill behind the Greenbelt Youth Center that rolled out onto Braden Field. It was perfect for sledding because it was so steep and yet there was nothing to wreck into. When Nik was 5, we had a huge snowstorm. We brought her friend Leila Knoll and her little brother, Dillan, who Nikky affectionately called Dill-pickle, and their dad, Cliff, there to sled. It was one of the best sledding days ever. The snow was deep and soft and fun to wipe out in. At one point, Cliff sent me spinning down the hill in a round snow tube.

I felt my legs bump something, and suddenly, Dill was sitting on my extended shins, spinning on down with me. I could hear the others screaming and laughing at the top of the hill. Dill enjoyed the ride with glee. He seemed to think it was just part of our plan like we meant to do that. We could hear Nikky, Leila, and Cliff laughing with surprise as we ran back up the hill. When we got up there, Dill was greeted with excited jubilation but, at the same time, with understanding that he didn't know he'd just been part of an amazingly entertaining accident. "Was that fun, buddy?" asked his dad. The snow was so deep and soft that the climb back up that steep hill was quite a workout, but every time we went down, we ran back up, excited to do it again as fast as possible. We did this for hours. Afterwards we went to Generous Joe's in the nearby Roosevelt Center for hot chocolate and sandwiches. It was an absolutely perfect day.

We were still using them when Nikky and Evan were dating. The Sled-Raft was my favorite back yard pool raft to just lay on and float peacefully in the summer. It was so cushiony and stable. I left it drying by the pool one day, and A-line winds, blowing at over 50 miles per hour, swept it into a tree and ripped it wide open. It was not repairable. I was so upset because brick-and-mortar toy stores had all but disappeared. I searched and searched but there were no more Sled-Rafts in any stores. I didn't realize how often I brought it up, but I mourned that raft out loud for the rest of the summer. Sure, I had the kind shaped like a chair with armrests and cup holders, but it wasn't the same. I couldn't turn on my stomach in those. I was also worried about not having it in the winter.

That Christmas, Nikky, Evan, and I were downstairs by the tree with a cozy fire exchanging gifts. My main gift for Nikky was her sewing machine. My main gift for Evan was a pair of tennis shoes that had retractable skating wheels. He and Nikky still had a handmade-only rule about Christmas gifts between them, but she knew he really wanted them. She had watched him skating around a store happily in them. He saw the price and decided not to buy them. He kept rethinking whether he should go back and get them. He was not expecting them, and he lit up when he opened them! He put them on immediately and skated down the hall. Gracefully coming back to us backward gliding on his heels, toes up with a giant smile. He clicked the wheels up, walked across the carpet, and we continued exchanging.

After a while, they conferred with knowing smiles. Nikky giggled and said, "Open this one next." handing me a huge box. It was about 24"x 24" and 6" deep. It was beautifully wrapped. It was so heavy. I couldn't imagine what could be inside this box. When I ripped it open, I GASPED!!! I could NOT believe it! A VERY high-pitched "WHAT!!!" squeaked out of my throat."OH MY GOD!" "OH MY GOD!" I screamed as I jumped to my feet, holding it up. "THE SLED-RAFT!!!" "It's the Sled-Raft!!" They just kept laughing as I jumped around. They were looking at each other, proud of this truly amazing Christmas surprise. "THANK YOUUUUU!!!" Where did you GET this???" I kept asking. Finally, Nikky said, "Evan found it online." I was not yet comfortable shopping online myself. This was one of the sweetest gifts! Normally, I had some idea what I might get for Christmas, but they did not give me one single clue, even though they were so excited to give it to me. I had just worried out loud about no sled raft for the winter days before. How they kept poker-faced through that I do not know. That was one of the best

Christmas surprises I have ever had.

    We used it year after year. Even Nikky's dog, Kairi, rode it between Nik and Evan down a hill behind the Library. The dog was so excited and would run to get back on over and over. There was a snowboarder there with us. When he left, we found he had made a fun, bumpy, winding track in the deep snow with a little jump at the end. We added snow to the jump, making it steep enough to get us airborne. It was so much fun! I still use the Sled-Raft in the pool to this day.

ORIGAMI FLOWERS

Nikky was probably 17 when she discovered a love of Origami. She made so many unbelievably beautiful creations. We would go to Joann Fabrics, and she'd pick out the thick papers for the creation she had in her head at the moment. She made lampshades for candles in wine glasses. She made castles and critters and even 3d 'Harry Potter' bookmarks of the Slytherins, Ravenclaw, Hufflepuff, and Gryffindor. Her creations were quite detailed.

On a Saturday before Mother's Day, she and Evan came home from Joann Fabric and said that they were not to be disturbed. No peeking in her room. They were in there quite a while, so I knocked to offer dinner..."DON'T OPEN THE DOOR!" Their voices said in harmony. They came out for dinner and went right back to work. The next morning, for Mother's Day, I was presented with a huge bouquet of the most amazing origami flowers! They were arranged in a tall glass Ginger jar-shaped vase with a sheer deep purple sash that brought out the colors of the flowers. There was every color and all different patterns like the patterns used in clothing. They were shaped like huge lilies with long Origami stems. This was just the most spectacular bouquet I'd ever seen. "You'll have these every year! They won't die." She said, smiling as I marveled at their beauty. The flowers were given a special spot in the living room where I could see them from down the hall when I got up and walked out of my bedroom every day. I could see them when in the living room and the dining room too. She was so right. I look at them every single day. They truly seem to rearrange themselves for special occasions. They are such a beautiful gift that keeps on giving and giving. Each year, when other moms share their Mother's Day gifts online, I share my handmade flowers.

MISTAKEN SONG LYRICS

I think everyone on earth has misheard song lyrics at one time or another. I have many, many times. For decades, I thought Jimmy Hendrix sang, "Excuse me, while I kiss **this guy**." What Nikky heard was often so random and funny, though. She and I and eventually her friends would scream Nikky's misheard version of lyrics over the songs. One of the funniest was Macy Gray: 'I try to say goodbye, and I choke, try to walk away, and I stumble, I try to hide it, it's clear,' then Nikky heard, "**I blow bubbles** when you are not here."

When she listened to Dave Matthews Band's 'Crash Into Me,' there was the part where he sang in a taunting kid's way, 'I'm the king of the castle' and then, 'You're a dirty rascal' but Nikky heard "You're a **bit of an asshole.**"

Then there was Fallout Boys 'Drop a Heart, Break a Name.' For some reason, Nikky heard: "**You're a whore, break a nail**" Driving the kids back home from visits, we would play these songs and yell Nikky's version so loud. I'm not sure what other people in traffic thought of our version of Fallout Boys, but it was funny as heck to us.

I feel Nikky lived years longer because Evan was in her life. She got to become an adult. To graduate art school and have a career as a graphic designer. I always say I am so lucky I had her as long as I did. She had tried to explain her depression to me in first grade. I had told her then, and I had complete confidence in this, that we'd find the right doctor and right therapy for her, and she was not alone. I thought you go to a doctor and find the right pills and all is well. Not by a long shot. We tried. I started taking her to therapists very young. She did not really let them see her depression, though. She was so used to hiding it. She was an expert at that as well. She was not going for the talk therapy, but she tried every therapy and every drug and drug combo available at the time. There are more available now. The combo of bipolar with anxiety she had was so difficult because when we treated the depression, it brought on upswings and anxiety at the same time. When we treated the anxiety, it brought debilitating depression. She tried homeopathic meds., including the sunlamp, but that gave her anxiety attacks. She tried hypnosis, exercise, meditation, I could go on and on. She was always looking for the next treatment. The drugs, like a lot of things, made her feel worse. So much so that she did something dangerous and stopped on her own. She didn't tell me. She was 14. I was driving her and her first boyfriend, Joe, to a movie. They rode in the back seat. I suddenly realized she'd been doing well for a longer-than-usual stretch. I looked in the rearview mirror and said, "NIkky, this is your third good week in a row doing well! She and Joe glanced at each other like they had a secret. That's all it took. **"NIKKY! Did you stop taking your meds??"** She quietly and calmly, with self-assurance, said, "Yes, I did, Mom, and I'm better without them." I decided then to support her in what she felt helped the most.

    Before taking her to doctors, what I didn't understand was that getting into her head was by invitation only. I also did not know how hard and sometimes impossible it can be to find the right combination of treatments. She only ever truly let 2 people in on those struggles, and that was me and later Evan. She didn't want to burden people, but also she wanted to pretend to be cheerful because she said that was when she felt best. She felt if friends and family really knew her struggles, they'd look at her differently, and it would always be there. No living in moments without the dark cloud in the background. So she pretended. She also felt best when she comforted others who suffered. She did not even let them in on her struggles. When she was 14, before she met Evan, she saw a commercial for a new birth control pill. It claimed to help with mood swings and cramps. She suffered terrible cramps as I did. She asked me if we could try it. We did, and that pill did everything it promised. It really helped level her moods. She stayed on it for the remaining 7 years of her life. All meds that help with depression or mood swings, including this one, have the possible side effects of depression and suicidal tendencies. All of them. I will not injure the people who may be helped by this pill by giving its name. It helped her. Still, she had unbearable depression and anxiety at times, but it was less often and much shorter lived.

Nikky's Note

JOHN HENRY

Greenbelt has a lot of character. It isn't perfect, that's for sure but it's different than other towns. It's kind of like Mayberry, only with eccentric people blending right into it. It's one of the few places where a car held together with duct tape can sit next to a Porsche and no one cares whose is whose. You also can't assume the duct-taped car has a less wealthy owner. We just are who we are.

There is a Greenbelt Icon named John Henry. He worked at St. Elizabeth's Mental Institution back in the day. He is very friendly and cheerful. He whistles really loudly in the Co-op grocery store, so I always know when a John Henry hug is coming. He would ask about Nikky and Evan every time he saw me. He was interested because he had something in common with the young couple. He is black, and his wife, Elaine, of many decades was white. It was kind of like he was rooting for this young biracial couple as well as the many other biracial couples he knew.

The historic part of Greenbelt has the benefits of a small town. Small towns have a way of stepping up when parents have to step back. That is what John Henry did for me. Every parent has a story like this, and every parent has also been on the other end of it when they themselves were young.

Nikky and I loved Halloween. When Nikky was young enough to Trick-Or-Treat, I used to dress up too and go with her. A lot of parents in Greenbelt did, too. When she got too old for that we started having Halloween parties.

One year, when Nikky was 16, we had a Rocky Horror Picture Show party and everyone dressed as a character from the movie. Nikky was Magenta. I was 'Dammit Janet.' We even had the sweet transvestite from Transylvania, and he was 6'3". I greeted people as they arrived with a newspaper on my head, saying I had a flat tire and walking them in the door. Nikky and friends LOVED Rocky Horror. Nikky played the song 'Timewarp,' and they all sang it at the top of their lungs while doing the dance. Nikky's Friend from French Immersion, Aimee, did her version of the solo tap part, which made me laugh so hard it's all you can hear in the video. In the end, like the actors in the movie, they all fell down as if they'd suddenly been unplugged. Later, it morphed into a costume DDR party, which made great photos.

Eventually, when she didn't want to have a party anymore, we made a huge deal of carving pumpkins together. We would excitedly plan our theme in advance. We drew our own patterns. One year we did 'Nightmare before Christmas'. Nikky loved all things Tim Burton. I did Jack in front of the moon. It was tricky with the skinny legs but came out awesome. Nikky did Sally. She was in graphic design at Eleanor Roosevelt, so as you can guess, hers were amazing. When the Trick-Or-Treaters came, we played the music from the movie. 'This is Halloween' could be heard up and down the street. It was a big hit with the kids and parents.

The town has a strong sense of community about it. That includes many family festivals. One festival is Pumpkin Carving. They put tables up in the Roosevelt Center, which is kind of the "Town Square." Everyone gets together with the pumpkins and tools at the tables and carves the Friday before Halloween. I never went because Nik and I did that together. This

Nikky's Note

particular year, I believe Nikky may have been 17. She informed me she and Evan were going to the festival to carve pumpkins. This did not come with an invite for me. Trust me, at that age, I understand wanting to be an independent couple carving together and not Ginger's kids carving with mom. I really do. So while I was disappointed for myself I was also happy for them. Still I was worried about my own pumpkin carving. Would I be doing it alone from now on? I would do it because I still love it, and I had many Trick-Or-Treaters but it would feel weird. I was shopping in the Co-op, and they had pumpkins. As I looked at them, thinking, "Should I get one, or should I get two?" I heard a loud musical whistle. I knew John Henry was approaching. I explained my pumpkin dilemma to him. "Get two!" he told me with confidence.

After the pumpkin carving festival, Nikky came home, and I asked if she had a good time. "It was great!" She said. John Henry sat with me and Evan! Can you believe he is almost 80 years old? He is so nice. Our pumpkins will be on display on the ghost walk tomorrow night that goes along the path to Northway Fields!" Then she asked, "Which night will we be doing ours?"

APPRECIATING CAMPING

Nikky would learn to appreciate camping. That was because of Evan. He was a Boy Scout. Also he and his dad went camping at the beach every single year. He was an expert camper, and he loved it. Growing up as a teen, I had gone camping with my brother, an Eagle Scout, and his friends in Paw Paw, West Virginia. Later, I went there with my future husband. I loved the stars at night. Away from the city lights, you could see so many stars. It felt 3D, like you could reach up and grab them. I also loved the perspective on life it gave me. The trees, the sky, and the lack of city made me feel so small and so peaceful. I was talking about that with Evan when he had just gotten back from a 2 week long Boy Scout backpacking trip in Philmont. Nik was listening. I spoke about the views of the stars in PawPaw, West Virginia. Evan asked, "Can you take me and Nikky there?" Nikky wanted to go because Evan wanted to go. So we went, and we had a beautiful weekend, cooking on an outdoor fire and hiking to the beautiful river. We visited the huge empty pool where the steam engine trains used to get water. We hiked to and climbed the fire towers, where you could view all of the mountains around.

In Paw Paw, trains would go through a tunnel in the mountain and then out onto a trestle over the river. We were walking in the live tunnel where trains still travel. I think this part of the trip struck Evan the most because a train came, and we jumped into the cubicles, which were cut into the tunnels for the workers to duck into when trains passed. The train runs right in front

Nikky's Note

of you. The sound of the train is deafening, and the vibration thumps into your chest. The wind is like a hurricane. You feel like you are being pulled into the train. It feels like it's inches from your face. It truly is actually only feet away. Then, as it exits there is a huge wind through the tunnel that you could almost fly on. Evan jumped up onto the track and put his arms out like he was flying, letting the wind in the tunnel fill his jacket like a kite. Nikky joined him. I felt so happy in that moment that they got to experience that. At night, we went back again and went out on the trestle which is the bridge over the river outside of the tunnel for the trains. You are elevated over the river. There are no trees blocking the view of the stars. It was the quietest Nikky ever was, just taking in the view of the stars. When they got older, Nikky and Evan went camping together at the beach. I was not there, but Evan took beautiful photos of the trip. Nikky's face, as well as her whole body expressed such a peaceful feeling. The same feeling I had when camping.

GRAPHIC DESIGN

I am always thankful my daughter grew old enough to have her career. It was for a short time, about 2 years, but I always would have wondered if she hadn't made it that far if being an adult and no longer in school and doing something she was great at would have helped with her depression. It didn't.

She actually did not intentionally choose Graphic Design; It was a happy accident. She had always taken art, but somehow, as a senior, she also got enrolled in the Graphic Design at Eleanor Roosevelt. She went to the guidance counselor to change it, but there wasn't a class for her at the same time, so she would have had to change all of her other classes to get out of it. She had lots of classes with her friends that year, as well as lunch, so she decided to suck it up and stay in the graphic design class. It actually seemed to challenge her. She told me the teacher was quite a perfectionist. The first person to tell me of Nikky's talent wasn't that teacher. It was our next-door neighbor who had gone to French Immersion with Nikky. Michael had chosen Graphic Design to be his future college major at a young age. He was in Nikky's graphic design class at ER, and he told me that he thought he had exceptional talent until he saw Nikky's work. When he saw her work, he decided he needed to pick a different major. That really stuck with me, but she had so many talents that I just sat back and let her find her path on her own.

Nikky came home after school one day and said the art teachers had

Nikky's Note

chosen her for a $2,000 Scholarship for art school. Three teachers were on the team that chose someone. Mrs. Thomas - Nikky's art teacher, Mr. Creek – photography, and Nikky's graphic design teacher. Mrs. Thomas told Nikky that all three teachers were arguing, saying that once the other two saw their student's work, they would choose their students. As it turned out, all three were talking about the same student. Nikky Brown.

She chose to go to art school. That was no surprise. She chose 'The Art Institute of Washington.' It was associated with The Art Institute of Atlanta. The AIA had been around for over 40 years. There were 7 prestigious art colleges associated with AIA scattered across the country. She decided to major in Graphic Design. They had a culinary school and also Fashion Design there. She took fashion design classes as well. She never made much of this, but she got a job online designing clothes that went to a runway show. Some people are probably wearing clothes right now that Nikky influenced. She also illustrated a kind of tween-aged book about twins. She entered a contest for artists to design a stuffed animal. Among hundreds of competitors, Nikky's furry-friendly purple monster was chosen. He was mass-produced and sold to kids. I have the original. She got to do so so much in her 21 years here on Earth. Again, it was as if she lived her life on fast forward. Like she knew time was limited, and she had so much to give.

One of her Graphic Design teachers at the Art Institute gave the class an assignment to do a stop-motion video. That's where it is a video of still shots that move around without showing feet move, etc. Like the old 'Mr. Bill' show from SNL. Nikky's started with her trying to play a game with her dog. She was waiting for the dog to take her turn when she fell into the game board. That's when the world became a cartoon. At first she was swimming in water with all kinds of fantasy things passing by. In the cartoon, she met Evan. In the end, she takes his hand, and they jump back into the real world together. And then she had a human to play the game with. She was working on it on a computer in the library at the Institute. There were only a couple of computers capable of doing what the students needed, so they were waiting hours in lines behind each other, seeing each other's work. When the students saw Nikky's they got intimidated. Nikky didn't know until it was time to show the videos in class. One student stood up and asked the teacher to please watch his **BEFORE** she saw Nikky's because Nikky would make his look lame. After that all of the students asked the same. The teacher agreed to watch Nikky's last. It was 2 or 3 days of videos. When the teacher finally saw Nikky's video, she said, "Nikky, one day when you are famous, will you please tell people that I was your teacher?" I wish I knew her name because I'd certainly keep Nikky's promise for her.

The way the school enrolls students is for an AA degree that, once you graduate, you can extend into a bachelor's degree. In order to graduate with the AA and move on, you have to do a portfolio demonstration of all of your work in front of 3 judges. The judges are professional art experts and are strangers to the students. They had one who was kind of a Simon Cowell type back when Simon played the meaner judge. Part of the judging is that you have to be dressed professionally as if you were in a job interview. Nikky did not normally dress that way as I am sure a lot of the artists didn't. She also didn't like the drive to the school, so she took Metro, as did a lot of the students. Metro in this area sometimes had trouble with the AC and they got really, really hot. I could not drive her. I had a patient in the office where I now worked that I couldn't miss. So 19-year-old Nikky, dressed in a Calvin Klein office dress and Kitten-heeled pumps that she never would have worn by choice, had to schlep her giant artworks on the metro just across the DC line to Arlington, Virginia, in a hot Metro rail car.

The boy who presented in front of her was in a suit, but it had gotten sweaty and wrinkled. The Simon Cowell like guy stopped him from showing any of his work and said he was not presentable for a job interview and he had failed. That meant no AA degree for him. Nikky told me she was so scared and nervous as it was suddenly her turn. She wanted to cry for the boy. They give the kids a score of 1 to 5. In the 40-plus years of the chain of school's existence, no one had ever gotten a 5. You had to get at least a 3.6 to pass and get your degree. Nikky got the highest score the school had ever given out, a 4.9. At this show there are talent scouts and business owners looking for artists to hire. They immediately approached Nikky and started competing to get her to come to join them. She had planned on continuing school. That morning, she thought she'd be a student for 2 more years. She couldn't answer such a question on the spot, so they all scheduled her interviews. It was the opposite of normal interviews. It was the interviewer trying to get Nik to come on board.

She actually chose the first job because of their needs. They had multiple mistakes with everything on their website including their logo. She worked there a while until she fixed the problems and then she started looking for an organization more devoted to charity. She found 'Good360,' and it was exactly the kind of work she wanted to do. Good360 is all about charity, as they use their diverse network to distribute essential goods to the people who need them. Things like repurposing "expired" mattresses, for example. A store can only sell mattresses until a certain date, and then they expire. Good360 got such mattresses to a Native American reservation where there were no beds. They also advertised for animal rescues, which Nikky loved. They did a lot of very wonderful things. They still do. So Nikky planned on taking this job. The people in the office where she had been working adored Nikky. Her boss immediately offered Nikky more money, not just a little, a LOT more. Nikky had to think about it. I told her to tell the Good360 boss what was happening. Well, Good360 offered her even more. This was not making it easy for her. We sat at the table, and she said she really wanted to work at Good360 but "What if the other one offers me some crazy amount of money?" I said. "Nikky, it is so important that you love your work. More important than the money. Tell the boss at the other office to understand that you want to do the charitable work and to please be happy for you and let you go." When she did, the boss cried. She understood, but she didn't want Nikky to go. She told Nikky that she herself had made the same choice for the same reason when she came to the company. She told Nikky she was sad for herself but happy for Nikky. These people actually came to Nikky's service. Both companies did. It made me feel so good that they loved her so much and valued her.

NIKKY'S HAIR

Like me, Nikky was born blonde. She had long blonde hair until she was 12. We had just moved into the new house, and she was ready for a hair change. "Could you cut my hair?" She asked. "Sure," I said. I'd been cutting my own hair since being pregnant with her. I got morning sickness from the smell in salons. I discovered then that I do a better job than I'd ever gotten by a professional. Nikky wanted her hair cut shorter than shoulder length but longer than her chin. I convinced her to do shoulder-length first and then wait a bit, and I'd cut it shorter if she still wanted. The worst feeling is when you cut your hair short and regret it. I didn't want that to happen. A couple of weeks later, she told me she was absolutely sure. Nikky loved her new hair! I was so happy watching her playfully swing it around as she sat on the couch in the new house one day. I took her pic, and we framed it. She looked so mature, and she liked that too. When she was 14, her short term boyfriend had a sister with her hair dyed red. She asked if she could dye hers.

I didn't let Nikky go to things like concerts or go to the mall and hang out without me. As I said previously, having Nikky, I realized not every kid needs the same parent. Nikky didn't like chaos. Things like that gave her terrible anxiety. She didn't even like 'Shenanigans.' She liked things orderly and controlled. She even had a hard time with kids with bad table manners. I knew if she went to concerts or the mall, she would likely not have a good time, and she could even be somewhat traumatized. She didn't ever argue with me, not letting her do these things. In fact, when I offered to take her instead of her going alone, she always appreciated it. But I did want her to be able to express herself and act like a teenager, too. So, I decided to allow her freedom with her hair and clothes. Again, wanting to start conservatively, I said, "How about maybe bangs and tips?" She liked the idea, so her bangs and tips were black against her blonde hair. She eventually started with more fun colors.

Nikky and friends loved Anime. There was a convention at the Baltimore Convention Center called Otakon. The kids dressed as Anime characters. With crazy hair colors, big boots, black suits, and swords and lasers, they were a little frightening to some of the tourists in town. That was ironic because these kids were all self-proclaimed nerds and gamers. Nikky asked me to take them because they were 14 and could not yet drive. I drove her and 2 friends, and we all went to the convention. They were dressed up. I was not. Nikky had dyed her hair purple and was dressed as a kitty with purple hair and ears, AcchiKocci. She looked really cute. She was less frightening to the tourists, who were confused about why they were seeing so many teens in costumes in the middle of summer. As we walked to a restaurant for lunch, one after another, they got brave enough to approach the cute Kitty with purple hair and ask what was happening. Nikky would kindly and excitedly explain to them about the convention and the Anime characters. It was nice to see them get so relieved and then show interest in the kids and the costumes once they understood

This may be a coincidence, but she was taking a photography class at Roosevelt. She had the same teacher I had, Mr. Creek. Anyway she was using a photo of herself and viewing it in all different colors. She was still blond at this point. In the photo, the wind had blown her hair all around her, framing the silhouette of her face with her turned-up little nose. She was changing only the color of the hair around her porcelain white face. She did deep blue, purple, orange, and then red. She was flipping through the colors on the computer in the basement while I pedaled the stationary bike. When I saw the red, I said, "Nikky, I want to paint that one. Can you print it?" She replied, "Oh, it's nothing. I'm just working on an assignment." "I want to paint that." I insisted. She printed it. I painted it. Then I painted it again making her a little older. I painted it a third time. Her dad came over, and he wanted one of the paintings, so I gave one to him. I framed and hung one. When relatives came over, they loved it and asked for one, so I made copies. After Nikky went through a few different colors, she died her hair the brilliant red in the painting. She loved it and kept her hair that color for the rest of her life. Life, art. Art, life? It was quite striking on her with her white skin and emerald green eyes.

When she was 20, she and Evan went to her first concert. She asked, and I said yes, but I warned her that it might be a bit crazy. She felt ready, and I felt safe with Evan there. So, they went. Evan ended up "crowd surfing," and they got separated. She couldn't see him; he was too far away, and she panicked. She tried calling him, but he couldn't hear the phone. He then called her, but they couldn't hear each other. They texted and found each other. When Nikky came home, I asked if she had fun. She started crying as she told me what happened. I told her it was good they could text and reconnect, and she'd know what to do next time. Turned out there wouldn't be a next time. She never asked to go to a concert again. As a kid, I had taken her to Jimmy Buffet, and she had a great time, but of course, mom was there so that was different. If you know teens who go to concerts with their parents, they may feel the same way she did.

Nikky's Note

Her love of reading

Late one night, I realized I had forgotten to rotate the laundry into the dryer. It was around the corner from Nikky's room. It was a school night, so I snuck down the hall as quietly as I could so as not to wake her. To my surprise, as I got near her door, I heard her voice. It came in the familiar rhythmic sound of someone reading aloud. As I got closer, she stopped, and I froze. Then I heard, "Are you asleep yet? Evan? Ok, good night." It was so sweet to know she was reading him to sleep on the phone. It reminded me of reading her to sleep every night when she was little.

She was always an avid reader. She would have me read the same books so that we could discuss them. I guess I was her book club. I am so thankful for that because I read so many books I would have missed out on. My favorite books are adolescent sci-fi. Always have been. It turned out to be her favorite as well. I didn't want to read 'Hunger Games' because I don't like violence or suffering, especially of kids. It wasn't a well-known book, never mind a movie yet, and she absolutely insisted I read it. "I don't think I can stand reading about kids fighting to the death, Nik," I said. "Please, mom. Just remind yourself it's not real and read it. At least try." I did, and of course, I was hooked immediately. It did bother me but I am so glad I read it. As it got better and better now. She got me to read so many wonderful sci-fi books. 'The Giver', 'The Uglies, The Pretties and The Specials' (trilogy), and 'The Girl with the Dragon Tattoo' etc. So many great books. She also got me to read 'The Book Thief'. That one was prefaced with a similar conversation about my concerns, but by then, I knew if she was asking me to read a book, it would be a good one. It became my favorite book of all time. She read aloud to Evan often. I have a beautiful photo of her framed, where she is reading 'Grass for his pillow' aloud to Evan on a picnic. Evan is a great photographer, and he took many poetic photos of Nikky.

Nikky's Note

NIKKY BREAKS THE NEWS OF HER SEXUAL ORIENTATION

From first to eighth grade, I went to Catholic school. I had lost my brother to SIDS before he was baptized. I was barely three years old, but when I heard my mom tearfully discussing with a friend that he may not be in heaven, I interrupted. "Wait, why isn't my brother in heaven?" I asked. They told me that when one dies without being baptized, it is believed that they don't go to heaven or hell but just stay in 'limbo.' At that age, I questioned things. So, of course, I really thought this one through. I thought, "So God gives you a baby. God takes that baby through no fault of anyone's. God then punishes the baby for eternity because he was taken too soon?" Nope. Clearly, they had this one wrong. And so it followed for me that if they got this one wrong, they probably had a lot more things wrong, too. I took comfort in the rituals and traditions and lifelong friendships formed in Catholic school. I was inspired to be good. I took comfort in God and heaven. However, I easily threw out anything that did not make sense to me.

So, I decided I would not force a certain belief on my own child. I would tell what people believed when asked and let my child decide for his or herself. One of the things I had tossed out as untrue was that God had a problem with people being Gay or Bi. When Nikky was about 4 years old, she asked me: "Mom, can a boy marry a boy?" "A boy usually marries a girl, but yes, a boy sometimes marries a boy," I said. End of discussion. A week later, "Mom, can a girl marry a girl?" Same answer. Nikky was extremely accepting. Later, when she went to Roosevelt, she was on the Gay Straight Alliance. Nikky had many Gay and Bi friends. I always let her know I would support her if she herself were Gay or Bi. Then, she started dating boys.

I was doing the dinner dishes when Nikky came up the steps. "Mom, I have something to tell you." She said. "I'm not gay." My hands stopped, and I turned to her. "Not even Bi?" I asked. "No, Mom, I'm straight." She said. "Ok," I said. "That is fine, Nikky. I just want you to be happy." I said. Then I paused and, imitating my mom's Bronx accent and exaggerated hand motions (for comedic effect), I said, "Although, I was thinking if you were Bi, you'd have a lot more options." We both laughed, and Nikky bounced back down the steps.

"Did you tell her?" I heard Evan ask. OK, so my daughter was straight. Not that there's anything wrong with that.

Nikky's Note

NIKKY AND EVAN BROKE UP

Tuesday, December 13th. Crappy things seem to fall on Tuesdays in my family. Nikky and Evan broke up. She came home and walked down the steps towards her bedroom. I'd been waiting for her. I met her in the hall. We looked at each other with tears in our eyes and hugged. "I love you," I said. "I love you too, mom." We both knew everything was going to be different, but I didn't realize it was the beginning of the end of my 21-year-old daughter's life.

Like the song 'How to Save a Life,' I stayed up all night with her in her room watching movies on her laptop. I had to work the next day. I texted a 'heads-up' that my daughter had broken up with Evan and was suicidal, so I'd be bringing her in with me. They knew both Nikky and Evan through me but hadn't met either. There was a big framed photo of Nikky and Evan in the room where I scanned patients. There was also a photo of Nikky holding Kairi. Alex from the front desk texted back, "Should I remove the photo?" His thinking of this made me so aware of how well they knew us. Nikky, who was now 5'8" and strikingly beautiful, came into the office with me. They were so kind to her. The doctor told her that her mom was very proud of her and that they all felt like they knew her. The patients also felt honored to finally meet her in person. But she couldn't stop crying.

I will never forget working on processing a patient's images and, out of the corner of my eye, seeing her red hair touching the floor. She was sitting in a chair I used for the patient's family to sit in so they could be in the room during their scans. She was folded in half with her stomach on her legs, hair touching the floor, and tears hitting the floor. A doctor she'd gone to in the past was in the building. I asked the staff to inform the doctor about what was happening. She called and asked if Nik would come to her office. Nikky's eyes got big, and she shook her head no. When I hung up, I said, "Nikky, you like that doctor. Let's go see her." "NO, PLEASE, MOM! I can't. Not right now. I'll go later." She said, and I believed her.

As days went by, Nikky kept refusing to go to her or any doctor. I still have texts in our old phones:

Me: Nikky, you were only 13 and 14 when we tried antidepressants. You are 21 now. It could be different this time. Why not try again?

Nikky: Because they not only didn't work but made me so much worse when I had full faith in them. I'm not willing to go through all of that again.

Me: Well, we should at least go to the beach and look at the ocean. You always feel good there looking at the waves and making sandcastles and collecting seashells.

Nikky: It's way too cold for the beach, and I feel like nothing, not even the beach will help me.

Me: How about hypnosis? We could go see my friend Dr. Grenzer again?

Nikky: Hypnosis helped your dirt phobia, but it didn't work for me.

Nikky's Note

I guess I should explain I had a terrible fear of those big orange piles of dirt on construction sites. When I had to drive out to Front Royal to see my sister, we passed an endless construction sight. I'd get anxious, and my hands would sweat, and I'd complain out loud until we got past it. There was always traffic there, so it was a lot of complaining.

Of course, Evan, who worked construction, found it funny, so one day, he sent me a pic of a pile of dirt. I sent him a text version of a 'Yell-o-gram' with his name in all caps. He responded with LOL. The pic was ugly, but the dirt only freaked me out in person.

We went to see a doctor I used to work with at Mercy. He was a genius at hypnosis, using it at the hospital for all kinds of things. He even got a pregnant woman who couldn't stop throwing up to stop. He helped people with weight loss. He helped with quitting smoking too, but that was only 50% effective.

When we left his office, we had to walk past a construction site with piles of dirt. We got to the car, and Nikky said, "WOW, Mom! The hypnosis WORKED on you!" "How do you know?" I asked. She explained what we just walked past and I didn't even notice it. At the time, I just figured it was worth a try, but I became a firm believer.

So, Nikky had decided not to seek treatment. I know some must be thinking, "Why didn't I force it? Baker Act her." I played that out in my head multiple times. It never worked, and it ended in disaster every time. As I said before, as far as anyone, including doctors, the way into Nikky Brown's mind was by invitation only. She would quickly have said all the right things and convinced them she was fine. And then it would have taken away the one person who really knew her. The one person she needed the most to have any chance to survive this. Me. Her mom. If she couldn't do that this time and they saw her as a threat to herself, they may have confined her. Like myself, that would have completely freaked her out. She would have had terrible anxiety attacks. They then would have to sedate her. The whole thing would have been absolute torture. I couldn't risk any of that. If I could go back in time I still would not do that to her.

    She did do some things to comfort herself, though. She seemed to have gotten to a place where she could survive. In hindsight, she had two plans. She was double-tracking. One plan included a future. She had bought new clothes. In fact, a new dress came later in the afternoon on the day she had died. She couldn't have known she'd be gone when she ordered it. Amy Wall later told me she was excited about the dress because it was not her usual style, but she was "branching out." She had gone onto a dating site for the first time in her life. She had even gone on what I would call a date with a male coworker from her previous job. I thought it was the beginning of getting better. At night, time for sleeping was her worst time. She had bought herself a sort of night light that projected stars and planets on the ceiling and all around her bedroom. She had a big stuffed dog to sleep with that she said gave great hugs.

    On New Year's Day, I discovered that the person I had been seeing for 3 months was still married. He had told me his wife left him with the kids years before. I texted Nikky. She was with her best friend, Amy Wall. "I'm with Amy at a diner. We will pay, and I'll be home." She said. When she got

Nikky's Note

home, she got her giant stuffed dog and handed him to me. "Give him a hug." She said. "Doesn't he give great hugs?" She was right. He gave great hugs. "You can sleep with him, Mom," she said. "Nikky, thank you so much, but you need your dog more than I do," I said. I later realized she meant when she wouldn't be here to need the hugs anymore, and I would need them more than ever.

She said things on different occasions that I later realized were meant for me after losing her. She had bought a whole new wardrobe of beautiful dresses and clothes for her new career. One day, she said I could wear her clothes. I said, "That is so nice of you, but I'd be afraid I'd wear something, and then you'd want to wear it for work." She said, "That won't happen." I asked, "How can you know that?" She just smiled and said. "I just know." She also said I could listen to her iPod. "Is there music on it I'd like?" I asked. "I think so," She said. Later, when I dared to listen, it was all heartbreaking songs. I kept thinking of her listening to them and feeling so bad. One was by Simon & Garfunkle, "Kathy's Song." It was so depressing. I guess to her, it was fitting. She told me I could use her computer. It was an expensive one which she had needed for graphic design. Again, I said, "Thank you, it's way better than mine, but I'd be afraid I'd mess it up or give it a bug like mine has." "No, it's protected." She said. Later I would get the photos of Nikky from her computer. I also was able to go onto facebook and tell her friends that she was gone.

Her friends believed surely she had been murdered. They only knew her as a ray of sunshine. I told them when I could get myself together, I would post her note. They all said, please do. I did. They then understood her. That note had the power to help the ones who loved her to understand.

Nikky always found it amusing that I love kid's movies. I prefer them to most adult movies. Violence bothers me in real life, and for me, I feel like movies should take me away from real-life things that upset me. I am OK with historical documentaries that are violent. It's gratuitous violence that is not for me. I had gone on a movie date with a person who I did not know was still married. When I came home, Nikky asked, "What movie did you see?" When I told her it was a James Bond movie, she was really annoyed. She knew I never would have chosen that. As it turned out a patient I'd gotten to know was the star. It made it fun to watch because Judy Dench was so nice and so friendly in person. It also made it so I knew the whole time that it was only a movie. Judy is fine. But we hadn't known that when we went because the date didn't know I knew Judy. Nikky went downstairs, and she and Evan discussed it. A few minutes later, Evan came upstairs and said, "The next time you two go on a movie date, you should see 'Wreck-it Ralph.'" I thought he was joking, but Nikky later said they meant it and that I'd love it. I didn't see it until after losing Nikky. When I did, I loved it so much, and I love them for knowing me so well.

Nikky's Note

MY GOODBYE

On what would turn out to be our last night together, Nikky wanted to get a special birthday present for her dad. He had suffered a traumatic brain injury while at work two and a half years before. She was going to visit him in the facility where he lives the next day. It would be a couple of days prior to his birthday. "I can't think of a good present." She said. I suggested a canvas and paint and brushes. We headed to Michael's Craft Store in the January snow. On the way, Nikky told me she was sitting on the Metro rail coming home from work that day. A wave of tears over her breakup hit her. She was unable to hide them from another girl in the car. The girl was a stranger who was close to her age. She did something amazing. She took one of her earbuds out and let Nikky listen to her music with her. She gave her some candy that she was eating. She let my daughter cry. That is something that is very hard for people to do. When Nikky told me this as I drove through the snow, the tears started streaming down my face. I couldn't stop crying, and Nikky did the same thing for me. She let me cry. I could feel her wanting to support me but forcing herself to allow the tears in silence. When we arrived at the store in Bowie, I couldn't get my eye makeup to look normal, so I just went inside looking like a mess. We had a good time selecting Charlie's gifts. We always had a good time in that store. On the way home, it started snowing really hard. I ran out of wiper fluid, which made it really hard to see. Nikky just quietly rode along, not acting scared or even annoyed. I was both angry at myself and white-knuckling the steering wheel as I drove. We stopped at Giant and got wiper fluid. Nikky rang it up in self-checkout. She had worked at Giant in school. She didn't want the night to be over. "When we get home, can we watch a movie together?" She asked. I have one I know you'll love. It's called 'How to Train Your Dragon.'" "Is it violent?" I asked. "No, it's a kid's movie." "Oh, ok. That sounds nice to me." I said. And she added, "We can paint our toenails with your new colors." She had given me a kind of Christmas stocking with fun nail colors in an effort to get me to branch out from my pinks and reds. One was a sea foam green that I loved. "We can watch in my room or the living room, you pick." She said. I chose the living room so that we could paint our nails more easily. I loved that movie, and I loved that time with my Nikky so, so much. I later realized it was the last good memory she wanted me to have. I have watched that movie and painted my toenails on that night every year since. I am so grateful she did that for me and I understand that she wants me to concentrate on the happy memories. I do. I really do.

Nikky's Note

LOSING NIKKY

The next evening, after she had visited with her dad, I asked if he liked the special birthday gift. She shrugged it off. She said she was going to the movies with Evan. She came home later, and I asked what movie they saw. "We didn't end up going." She said. "Evan doesn't feel well." She went downstairs for a short time. I was watching TV on the couch. When she came back up and said, "I'm going back to Evan's." "Even though he's sick?" I asked. "Yes." She said. I wish you'd stay home. It's not healthy." I said. "I know, Mom", she said. Those were our last words. That was the last time she walked out of our home on Lastner Lane.

BANG BANG BANG. The loudest knock came on the door. I was sleeping on the couch. I opened my eyes and looked at the wall clock. It was 3 am. I jumped up and came around the iron stair rail, confused. I looked down, and through the small rectangular window on our front door, I saw two shoulders touching. They were in police uniforms. I can't tell you how it felt. There aren't words. I knew they were not here to give me good news. As it turned out, they were here to give me the worst news any parent could ever hear. I knew Nikky would never break any law. I opened the door. I couldn't understand what they were telling me. I was so confused at first. They said that the body of a young female had been found along with my daughter's car in the Northway Fields dirt parking lot. The young woman had been shot.

"My daughter is the most peaceful person on earth," I told them. "She would never ever harm anyone."

"Where are your guns?" The tall, thin, dark-haired one asked. I thought they were trying to tell me Nikky had shot someone.

"I don't have any guns," I said. "I'm a no-gun person." I was too stunned to correctly word the fact that the only guns that had entered my home since we'd lived here were the ones they were wearing right now.

I understand people feeling safer with a gun for self-defense. I also know that once in a while, it saves a good person from a bad person. I personally have never wanted a gun in my house. I know they are most often used in regrettable acts of anger, by accident, or for suicide. I didn't want any in my house. Nikky knew this. She is not a rule breaker, so ironically, she kept her newly acquired gun in the trunk of her car so as not to break my rule. Another testimony as to who she was.

"What was your daughter wearing tonight?" The dark-haired officer asked. "I can't remember," I said. Then the other officer spoke so softly, "Black coat, Leggings, Boots?"

In a movie-like slow motion, my eyes turned away from the dark-haired officer, and I looked at him. We locked eyes, and I felt the blood drain from my body. I had the worst sinking feeling in my life. I felt my world collapse. I felt so weak. "Oh," I said. "That's Nikky........."

They were telling me the lifeless body with her car was... Nikky... My angel. The person I was the closest with on earth. My heart and soul. The person I loved more than life itself. The reason I lived. The one I loved more than myself. It was Nikky. I immediately thought I could not live through this. I didn't have a suicide plan. I just knew I couldn't live on.

I didn't make a conscious decision to sit down, but I just suddenly couldn't stand up anymore. I sat down on the steps. I leaned my head on the wall. I was so weak. Both officers became concerned, then. "Who can we call to come be with you?" The softer-speaking one asked. "No one," I said. "We should call someone to come over." He insisted. I couldn't process what was happening. I just needed to be alone and try to understand what I'd just been told. I tried to act like I was OK. "I don't want anyone here," I said. The soft spoken officer had recognized me from Eleanor Roosevelt. He kept looking concerned. The other officer asked about who else knew Nikky. "Does she have any enemies?" He asked.

"No. Everyone loves Nikky." "She had just broken up with her seven-year boyfriend and was suicidal." In my mind, the loss was explained. "What is his name? Where does he live?" I hesitated. "Ma'am, this is a murder investigation," said the dark-haired officer. They left. They were going to Evan's house next. The soft-spoken one, seeing my distress, offered to stay with me, but the other one ushered him out.

The door shut. I sat there frozen. I couldn't move, or maybe I didn't want to. I didn't want to go on and exist, so I just didn't move. It was like my brain gave me a break because I wasn't really thinking. I didn't even feel like I was breathing. I was just not being for a while.

I didn't know how long I'd been there. Still sitting on the steps, my head leaning on the wall, I spoke to my daughter. "I love you, Nikky, and I understand."

I got up and saw the living room wall clock. It was almost 4 am. That was bewildering to me. It had just said 3 am, what felt like 10 minutes ago, when the police had woken me. I picked up my phone from the charger on the kitchen counter. I texted my sister, Kathy. "Nikky's gone." She immediately texted back. "What?" I texted, "She committed suicide. The police just left." "I'll be right there." She texted. She lived in Front Royal. "I'll tell Mom and Dad so they can come be there with you." They still lived nearby in the house we grew up in in Greenbelt. "No." I texted. "I want to be alone." Thankfully, she ignored that request because, within minutes, I suddenly felt like I was going to go completely crazy. It was such an awful, scary feeling. I am no good with medicines, so I had nothing. I went to the fridge and poured a big glass of wine. It helped, but the feeling kept coming back. Suddenly, my door opened, and my parents were coming up the steps. My dad had had knee surgery and was pulling himself up the railing with both distress and determination on his face at the same time. My mom was right behind him. We sat at the table, and they kept talking about any and everything they could. I informed them I'd be drinking wine. They said nothing. We talked and talked, but I don't know about what. The table was in front of the sliding glass door that leads to the pool. We faced East. In time, I saw the light and colors of the sun rising. I felt like it was an insult. "How can the sun come up when Nikky is not here?" I asked. Both murmured in agreement. The sun had the nerve to keep making the yard brighter and brighter. Then I noticed something was floating on the water on the pool cover. It was a male and female duck. They'd never been here before. "There are ducks on the pool cover!" I said. My parents got up from the table and looked outside, too. I kept watching the ducks. I knew they were here to comfort me. The pool literally existed because of Nikky's Birthday parties.

BIRTHDAY PARTIES

The first house Nikky was born into was a GHI (Greenbelt Homes Incorporated), which is a Co-op. They were built as part of FDR's 'New Deal'. They are tiny row houses that were very affordable at the time. Greenbelters who grew up in them were used to the little homes. I grew up in one. We had 5 kids when my mom got divorced. We were in a 3-bedroom brick house. When my mother remarried, my new sister and dad joined us. Our parents wanted to move to a bigger house. My brother and I did not want to move. A neighbor suggested an addition instead of a move on top of all the new changes in our lives. That is what my parents did, and we stayed.

The size of our house didn't stop my mom from throwing giant sleepover birthday parties. Since we had 5 girls, although 2 were twins, that meant a LOT of birthday parties. So when I had Nikky in our 2 bedroom row house, it didn't stop me either.

She was 5 when we planned her first friends-only party. She was very excited. She had asked for a Barbie cake. I put my order in at Baskin Robins. Nikky was with me when we went to pick it up. I was so hoping she'd approve of their work. There were two employees, both black, a young male and a female. They were getting ready to put the top on the cake with their backs to me, and both started laughing. I waited patiently as they whispered and chuckled. The female turned and said to me, "Ma'am, we only have one Barbie cake topper left, and this is it." She presented a beautiful Barbie from the waist up with a long stem to be stuck into the bottom half of her huge

Nikky's Note

pink dress made of cake. She happened to be black, which is why they were laughing. "Oh, I don't think that'll be a problem," I said. "Put it in the cake." They did and brought it to the counter. It truly was stunning. Nikky was off looking at the cakes in a refrigerator. "Nikky!" I said with wonder in my voice, "Look at your cake!" She came over and looked and lit up. With a gasp, she said. "Ohhhh! She's BEAUTIFUL!!" We left happily with our cake. Later, when the cake was presented to the girls, they all were just amazed at the beautiful Barbie. I had to cut carefully around the bottom to preserve her as long as possible. She sat in the center of the birthday table, covered in different shades of pink. The tablecloth, the napkins, the plates, the cups, the forks, the steamers, the balloons, and the party hats all matched the pinks and white in her magnificent dress. She really added quite the 'Wow' factor. I don't think I've ever even seen a wedding cake as spectacular.

It became THE party that no girl wanted to miss. She was born on Memorial Day, so while the date of the holiday changed, her birthday was celebrated on Memorial Day weekends. That is when the Greenbelt pool opened, and going on the first day was like seeing a new movie on day one. You didn't want to miss it. I usually got one of the party guest's parent or sometimes a kind friend, to help drive all of the kids to the pool. They had an awesome day, and then we went back to our little house for cake and, presents and games. The first year we had it was when Nik was in kindergarten. I had not planned a sleepover. Two of the guests slept over regularly but never had at the same time. We had cake and ice cream and presents and were playing games when Leila, who slept over regularly asked if she could spend the night. I said yes if it's ok with your parents. We were in the kitchen, but again, tiny house the others heard. Maddy, our other regular sleepover, immediately asked, followed by the pleading voices of every other girl there. "Oooo, Can I sleep over, tooo??" So I had them all call their parents and ask permission and the parents happily brought sleeping bags and toothbrushes and PJs. Learning from my mom, I always had pasta and spaghetti sauce in the cabinet. I made a huge pot of spaghetti, both inexpensive and easy. The girls happily chatted while they ate their dinner. Then we polished off the Barbie cake and ice cream. We played games until they wanted to watch movies. Back then, I had an endless supply of Disney movies, which satisfied all. I always had microwave popcorn and movie snacks. I soon realized as I got sleepy that the girls would outlast me. They listened when I said if they stayed quiet, they could stay up. In the morning, they slept in as they had stayed up so late. If you don't know that trick, I highly recommend it. I had a waffle Iron and put that to work for breakfast.

After breakfast, the girls went out into the yard, playing and having fun with a jump rope, a ball, and the new birthday toys. Seeing the group of kids, the Ice Cream Man came to the driveway in his truck with his song playing loudly. Back then, it was only $1.00. All of the girls got ice cream. They were so excited. It was like Santa had come to visit! The Ice Cream Man never forgot to come to our court on Memorial Day Weekend every year after that. It was part of the party. The parents came to pick their kids up around lunch time and all had something to tell me about how they appreciated the time alone or on a date night. I realized then this would be our tradition. I truly enjoyed those parties. When the girls were older and still coming to the party at the new house on Lastner Lane with the pool, one of the girls told me that had been her first time ever having ice cream from the the ice cream man in her life. She had been so thrilled that she kept talking about it to her parents and siblings. Her parents then let them have ice cream from the truck each summer after that.

    Nikky and I always dreamed of one day having our own pool for her party and for ourselves. When she was 10, I left Mercy Hospital and got an office job as a Nuclear Med. Tech. I loved the new Job in College Park. It paid enough that I could save up and we moved a couple of years later to a split foyer house on Lastner Lane. It didn't have a pool, though. Nikky was now 12 and was having sudden unexpected crying at times. She had been seeing therapists, but they did not feel she was depressed. When I showed her the house, she happened to hit one of the crying jags in the large backyard. I misinterpreted it to be that she was sad about the lack of pool. We had looked at 2 houses with pools, but they weren't in Greenbelt. At the time, homes were increasing in value so quickly that I knew I could use equity to pay off a loan to put the pool in. I told Nikky we'd put a pool in ourselves, and we did. I have to say we took full advantage of the pool, having huge pool birthday sleepover parties. We also would host many weekend sleepover DDR (Dance Dance Revolution) parties. I had multiple family pool parties, too. I loved grilling poolside. I remember floating in the pool, thinking I wouldn't sell this house for any amount of money right now.

FINDING THE NOTE

My parents had sat back down at the dining room table. As the sun continued to rise, I was starting to realize that, ready or not, the next day was arriving. It was morning, even though it still felt like the middle of the night to me. I texted Evan. "I guess you know Nikky is gone." "Yes." he texted. "Did you find her note?"

"There's a NOTE?"

"Yes," he texted. "She said if she ever did this, it would be on her desk in her bedroom."

I jumped up, and as I flew down the first set of steps, my parents called after me. "Where are you going?" "There might be a note!" I yelled over my shoulder. I ran down the hall to her bedroom doorway. Her bedroom was on the West side of the house, so there was just enough light in the room to see it. There was a small envelope with a folded piece of loose leaf paper turned sideways so it was sticking out. I unfolded it and sat on the edge of her bed. I turned the light on. The note had her beautiful handwriting on both sides. As I read, it felt like Nikky was standing in front of me, extending her hand out and speaking words of comfort, love, and advice. I read it at least a hundred times that day and a million times more in the days and years to follow. I feel her love pouring out to me every time. It saved my life. I wouldn't go crazy now. I would take her loving advice and live for her.

Nikky's Note

Her Note:

> Mom,
>
> I am so sorry. I love you very much.
>
> You've been a wonderful mother, and you don't deserve this. I can't stress enough how much you and everyone else, shouldn't blame yourself or regret anything you did or didn't do toward me.
>
> What I wish everyone could understand is that I appreciate all the support and love and care I've been given. I've always been really fortunate in a lot of ways - but that's why I know I'll never get "better". Even with great people in my life, and even with a job I love and a future where I know I can achieve goals, I'm just not a happy person. My depression outweighs my best times. It has nothing to do with others, I could have everything I want, and living still wouldn't feel worth it. And I'm depressed enough right now to get out of it, and too scared of being miserable for another 80 years not to.
>
> I'm just so sorry for how it will

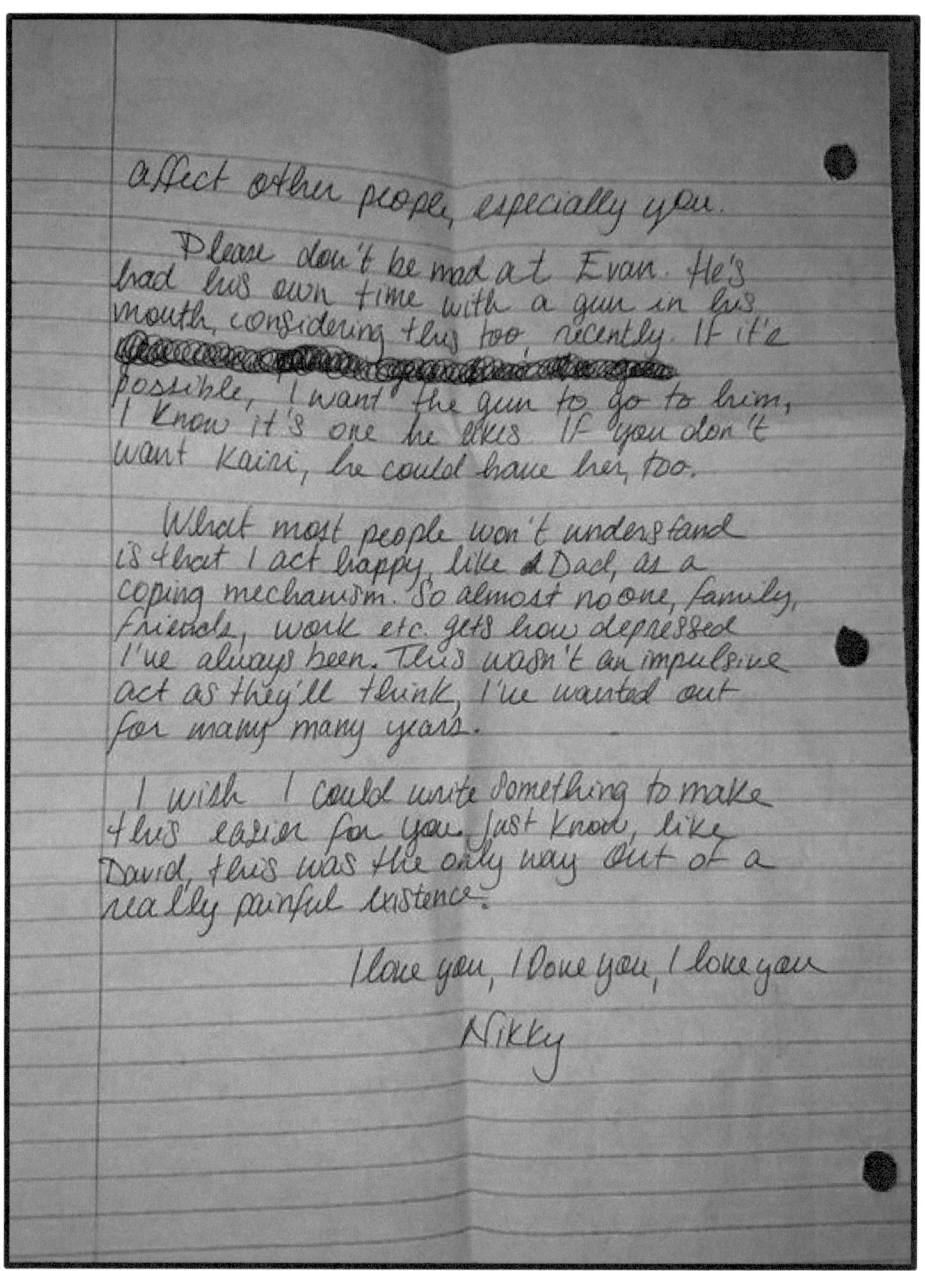

Nikky's Note

I kept thinking of the many people who've lost someone to suicide but with no note. I knew I needed to share her words with them, too. My friend Mary was one of those people. For the next few days, my house was continuously full of people. Every one of them read the note. It was Mary who I wanted to see it most. Her brother had taken his own life 2 years before, and she had asked herself daily things like, "Why? Could I have changed it?" and "Where is his note?" Since losing David, I had never had a conversation with Mary where she didn't ask those things. After she read Nikky's note, Mary never asked those questions again. She had actually scoured his home, even looking in between pages of books searching for a note that didn't exist. Nikky's note had brought my friend the comfort and understanding she was searching for. This is another reason I feel people who have lost someone to Suicide should be allowed to read Nikky's note. There are also people who feel angry at the loved one lost. I feel like my letting those people get to know and understand Nikky, and allowing them to read her note may change the anger into understanding and compassion.

My original thought was to get her note to people who needed the comfort of her words as fast as possible. I knew the owner of the Funeral home where we had Nikky's service. He knew me and he knew Nikky through my speaking of her for years. I gave a copy of her note to him telling him to share it with those who may find comfort in it. But that wasn't enough. There are people all over the world who have lost someone to suicide. Right after her death, my lifelong friends met me on a Sunday at 'Fishnet' in College Park for brunch. Some hadn't yet read the note so we passed it around there. They agreed it should be shared. One even shared a copy with her mom, who had lost her own mother to suicide. We just never came up with a perfect plan to share it with the world.

A year after losing Nikky, Robin Williams took his own life. When I saw on social media the reactions of people, I realized I was one of the few people who understood Robin. I understood him because I understood Nikky. The people asked over and over how one with so many gifts could leave Earth this way. I wanted to raise my hand as if in school and say, "Well, I get it. I know how and why". I knew I needed to share who Nikky really was with the world. They needed to understand her and, in doing so, understand the many people like my daughter and Robin Williams. Since her death, I have been writing what I call 'Nikkyisms' in little notebooks. They were for me. Things like: "You never cleaned your plate at a restaurant, and you always found a way to make a smiley face on the plate with the leftover food. The waiters always got a chuckle." Short Nikkyisms and long ones, too. Having written about her daily made writing this book feel natural. Most people do not leave a note. In fact, less than 30% leave one. That leaves a lot of people searching for answers and, worse, possibly blaming themselves.

The night I lost Nikky, my sister Kathy stayed with me. People had left, and we were sitting in the living room talking and I saw she was trying not to fall asleep. I looked at the clock and was shocked to see that it again was 3 AM. I had been awake for 24 hours, but I couldn't imagine going to sleep. Now, she also had been up for 23 hours, and I had to let her sleep. So I told her I was tired and went to bed. She had slept in Nikky's bed on other occasions, and once I went into my room, she went downstairs. I decided just to lay down, at least. As I closed my eyes, I heard what sounded like my mom's sister, Aunt Jackie, and my Uncle Bob yelling in my ear: "NIKKY IS OK. NIKKY IS HERE WITH US. NIKKY IS OK. NIKKY IS HERE WITH US." I opened my eyes. I was confused for a second, thinking my uncle was still alive. "Nikky isn't on Lakeside in their house," I thought. Then I realized my uncle had died a couple of years earlier. That wasn't my aunt and uncle. That was my grandmother on my mom's side, Grandma Schultz, and Uncle Bob telling me Nikky is Ok and she is with them. I never doubted there is more than this existence but hearing that from them was so so so very comforting. And it was so amazing too. I wondered how hard it was for them to get that message to me. I slept for a few hours but was up again.

HER SERVICE

Nikky and I had both wanted to be cremated. We had discussed it because I felt my family would disagree, but I wanted her to be able to say she absolutely knew it was what I wanted. That's when she told me she wanted the same. To both of us, being scattered in places we loved was happier than being in a box underground. Plus, I feel like watching that box go down into the hole in the ground is so dreary and sad and even unhealthy. I feel a sweet, happy service is better for the living. She was cremated. While I know she was there at her service, her ashes were not. An urn seemed too old lady-ish for her. She stayed in the plain white box that I received her in, which was in a little white bag with handles. I knew not to get all of the ashes from a friend who made that mistake in the past, so the bag was the size of a very small shopping bag. And a simple bag is much more Nikky than an ornate urn would be.

We had her service at Borgwardt, where my family and a lot of Greenbelters always go. She was not religious, so no Priest. We had a continuous loop slide show of photos of her life picked by the many friends and family who were in my house following the loss. I had drawers and drawers of photos, so everyone got to help and pick some out. We also had paintings she had done, as well as one I had done of her around the room. The flowers were very sweet and so thoughtful. And there were people. So many, many people.

Nikky's Note

A person from Nikky's beloved 'Good 360' walked up to me with love in her voice and a box in her hands. As she said kind words, the box was handed to me. It had no lid. I looked down into this box which immediately pulled me into Nikky's office life like a magnet. Her favorite giant 'Ninja turtles' mug was in it. There was a giant pencil with an anime character on it. Her Oscar the grouch critter and her cubicle photo in a plexiglass frame that told about her accomplishments and who she was. Her smile - so sweet and unassuming in the photo which was laid on top of the green apple signature color with their logo in black lettering. It told me so much at a glance. I couldn't stop looking. I was staring into the box when an unknown pair of hands appeared and gently removed the box from my hands. It felt like I moved from one world to another as I left her office and looked up to see a long line of people waiting to tell me of their connection to and love of Nikky.

I was so moved and happy to hear all of the stories and feel the admiration and love of Nikky from all of these people. It meant the world to me at a time when I needed it so very much. A group from her office walked up to me, and two women my age were speaking of everything Nikky did for them and how sweet and kind she was. Most of the others were around Nikky's age and were kind of hanging back a little, listening. One of the women said to them, "It's ok, come forward, don't be shy." They scooted closer and started telling me cute, funny stories of my daughter. I laughed, and the younger ones looked at each other, startled. "OH my GOODNESS! She even LAUGHS like Nikky!!" One gasped. Then I realized how strange it must be to come to her service and see an older blond version of Nikky standing there in front of them. But I loved it when people thought I look like my beautiful daughter. I never knew we laughed the same until that moment. It made me really happy. They made me happy.

My sister Kathy and I rode back to my house with my cousin. As we were parking, I could see through the living room window to the back sliding doors. The window was filled with the silhouettes of a huge crowd of people. Standing room only. I had been in a daze since the loss, but right then, I told my sister and cousin, "You guys, I'm having chest pain. I don't want to do anything about it right now I'm just giving you a heads up." They looked at each other. "OK." said my sister. My cousin came around to the passenger side and walked close to me, making small talk but looking concerned. When I got inside and near all of the friends and family, the chest pain disappeared. I'm so thankful and lucky those people were there. They kept me moving and talking and not feeling the stress. I saw on the coffee table, the box from Nikky's office. I still do not know whose hands took that box from mine or who delivered it here.

Nikky's Note

YOU WERE RIGHT

As I said, Nikky did not believe in a higher power. No God, No heaven. I am very spiritual, and I couldn't imagine that. We talked about it a lot when she was older. I'd ask her when we looked at the ocean or the stars, "When you look at that you think it's just an accident? It doesn't make you think there is a God who put this together for us?" No was always the answer. Our living room faced the West and had a giant window almost ceiling to floor. We were sitting at the table in the dining room which was all one big room. The sun was going down. This sunset was one of those amazingly beautiful ones with a symphony of colors in 360 degrees. We had the sliding doors facing the East, so we were surrounded by the beauty. "Nikky, I know what you are gonna say, but I just can't look at things like this sunset and not believe there is a God." I said, "I know there is more than just this existence, and when I die, I am coming back down here just to tell you that I was RIGHT!" I said with determination and a chuckle. She laughed and said, "OK, and if I die first and there is more than just this existence, I will come down and tell YOU you were right."

After losing Nikky, two of my sisters, Kathy and Kim, took turns staying with me until I was ready to be alone. On the first morning I woke up, I stayed in bed, as I often did. Then I heard a very welcome and familiar sound. Every morning before work, Nikky would climb our creaky steps and walk down the equally creaky hardwood hall to the full-length mirror outside my bedroom door. She'd pause, looking in the mirror, and when I heard her shift her weight to turn to leave, I'd say, "Have a nice day, Sweetie." She'd reply, "You too, Mom."

As I lay there this morning, I heard her unmistakable footsteps coming up from the landing and down the hall. I kept my eyes closed, afraid she'd disappear if I opened them. She stopped outside my door, as always, shifted her weight, and then leaned into the bedroom. "You were RIGHT!" She sang loudly into my room. I sat up so fast, expecting her to be there. "Nikky?" But my room was empty. "What was I right about?" I asked out loud. Then I realized she had kept her promise. There is more than this existence. I am so thankful that this wouldn't be the last time I heard from Nikky. I should have known that this gifted person would also be a gifted angel.

That evening, I was walking Kairi. We always walk at least 2 miles. As we were nearing home, I saw a little red bird on the sidewalk. It was not a bird I'd seen before. It was a little bigger than a sparrow. The bird was not moving off of the sidewalk. Kairi is a springer spaniel, also known as a bird dog. I figured as we got closer, the bird would fly off, but it didn't. We got so close that I stopped walking and held Kairi back. We were about 3 feet from the bird. "Excuse us," I said. The bird then flew up onto one of those metal lines with a fender over it that goes diagonally into the ground. The bird sat at my eye level a few feet away. I saw a white fluffy thing in its mouth. I stayed still, trying to figure out what it was. Suddenly, the bird shook her head like a dog with a toy. Dandelion seeds floated down all around us. "I know you are here, Nikky," I said to the bird. The little red bird then flew towards our house and out of sight. I opened the door and looked up at my daughter's life-sized self-portrait from an art school assignment. It was on the wall in the foyer. The wall is a story and a half, and that is the only wall tall enough for it. In the portrait, Nikky is in a dress blowing in a gentle breeze, standing in a field of fluffy white dandelions. She has one in her hand and is blowing the seeds into the breeze. Dandelions were Nikky's favorite flower. Now, they are mine.

EVAN AND KAIRI AFTER NIKKY

I was fortunate to have the support of not only family but also lifelong friends. A group decided to have a drum circle for me at a house on the Chesapeake Bay. It was a sleepover. I was reluctant to leave Nikky's (now my) dog, Kairi. She had terrible separation anxiety after Nikky died. All she knew was Nikky left and didn't come home. She would sleep on the landing with her back leaning against the door, waiting for her to come through it. I just couldn't imagine leaving her overnight by herself now. She didn't let me out of her sight during the day. There was only one person who she would get excited to see other than Nikky and that was Evan. I texted and asked if he could look after her while I went to the sleepover. He agreed immediately. He texted, "Sure, of course!" and a smiley. So I knew it wasn't just obligation or doing me a favor. He wanted to see Kairi and my little 6 lb Chihuahua, Oreo too. Evan became my go-to sitter and looked after Kairi and Oreo multiple times.

One of those times, I was away for an entire week with the group of lifelong friends. They had held a meeting and decided to go to Puerto Rico together in October. I had never left Kairi or Oreo for a week. I'd always brought them when I was away that long. I knew Evan worked days and couldn't do it all alone. I asked Nikky's best friend, Amy Wall to help. She agreed. I also had a friend who rented a room in a family's home. I knew it'd be like a vacation for him to stay in a house by himself, and it was close to his work. He agreed to stay over. We had it all covered. Evan knew how hard it was for me to leave the dogs for even a weekend, never mind a week. He texted me pics of the happy dogs daily. They were having walks, eating together from the same bowl at the same time as they always did, and cuddling on the couch. I waited to see those pics every day. It made the trip so much better. Of course, he has his sense of humor, so one pic was of Oreo pooping! I responded with my text version of a 'yell-o-gram' with his name in all caps. His reply was, "LOL." Then I told all of the girls about the pic because it was funny. I didn't show them the pic, though. Oreo would have been embarrassed!

Evan, like Nikky, always wanted to make people happy. He would actually become what he thought a person wanted him to be in their presence. He wasn't misleading them so much as just morphing into what they wanted. He loved Nikky so much and in her presence, wanted to be her partner forever. He was an artist. He was very talented. So much so that he got a scholarship to the Corcoran School of Art. He was an extremely talented photographer and sculptor and amazing at ceramics and anything he tried. In the presence of his dad, he was a construction worker/contractor. He truly is talented at that, as well. He was an expert camper and a Boy Scout and great at landscaping and growing vegetables. Around his mom, he was a Thespian, in plays with her, and a model in online commercials. His mom had wanted him to go to military school and he went along looking at one with her. With his sister, kind of a nerd, and that worked for Nikky too. With me, he was intelligent, sensitive, very funny and fun. He loved animals and nature. He was the person who really knew and loved my daughter and appreciated her. He understood her anxiety and was sensitive to her fragility.

He may think he caused Nikky's suicide. One incident did not take Nikky. Anxiety and bipolar depression took Nikky. She always had it hanging over her head. I feel Nikky lived years longer because Evan was in her life. I am so thankful she lived until 21 and got to have a career.

I'll never forget the night Kairi stopped waiting for Nikky. When Nikky left for work in the mornings Kairi would come join me and Oreo in my bed. Again, I was the third choice behind Nik and Evan. But once Nikky died, Kairi stayed in front of the door as she used to when Nikky was coming home late from work or going out.

It was three years after Nikky had died. Every evening a Honda that sounded exactly like Nikky's pulled up and parked in front of my house. Kairi would go bananas. Ears up, tail wagging, barking, panting, and running in circles, down to the door, back to the window. Down to the door, back to the window, thinking Nikky was finally home. She'd look at me, eyebrows up, and I'd shake my head and say, "No. It isn't Nikky." She understood, and her tail would sink. On this night, after three years of that routine, The Honda pulled up with its low putt-putt noise. Kairi picked her head up, ears perked up, looked at the window and then at me. I shook my head no. She put her head back down and kept her eyes on me and she relaxed. That night, when Oreo and I went to bed, Kairi came with us. She slept with us ever after. I hope Nikky was able to visit her and let her know they'll see each other again one day. In the meantime, I went from being her

Nikky's Note

grandma to being her mom.

SURVIVING I'LL GO FIRST

It's a sincere question, yet we can't ask it: "How do you go on?" "How can you live one more day, never mind years, after losing your daughter?" So people ask, "How are you?" And I try to tell them I am ok. I am so lucky to have an entire town of people who support me, as well as so many people who loved Nikky and came forward. The truth of this existence is that no one gets through it without suffering loss. Losing a child, though, is paralyzing, especially in a tragic and dramatic way. For those who have not been through that, it puts their losses into a different perspective but also makes them question, "How could one live through that? Could I live through it?" I will do my best to tell you how I have.

Before losing her, I thought I could not live through it. The first thing that gave me the ability to go on was her note. It literally kept me alive. It actually obligated me to live. She worked so hard to comfort me that I felt not going on or even sinking into a life of my own depression, would hurt my daughter. I was determined not to do that. Nikky and I had spoken to each other of how we wanted the good times of our lives remembered by our loved ones to outweigh the sadness of the loss in our death. However, I had thought I meant her remembering me after losing me. I took the advice meant for her. I chose to keep the beautiful memories of her held higher in my mind and to give them more power than the pain caused by the loss. It is a choice. It isn't easy. It will take a lot of work for the rest of my life.

Nikky's Note

Others who have lost a loved one to suicide may keep telling themselves things like: "I should have known." "I should have seen the signs." "Maybe if I had done this or not done that, maybe she'd still be here," I say this to you. I get it. Whenever I start to do that, I remember her last words and wishes to me. She wished me not to do that. I then tell myself, "NO! Nikky specifically told you not to do that." Her exact words were, "Do not regret anything you did or did not do towards me." Those words saved my life.

What I hope is that you can think of the person you lost writing or saying those words to you. They want you to cherish the time, however limited, that you had with them. Those times and that love is the gift you should focus on and be thankful for. The connection cannot be lost. They are still part of you and always will be. It won't go away.

As I've said, I am very spiritual. When I think of the mental pain and anguish my daughter suffered on earth, it is not something I can understand. Like so many things in this existence, it seems to be without purpose and cruel. There are two truths about being her mom that seem mutually exclusive, yet both are true at the same time. One is I am so very thankful I got to be this amazing person's mother. She is the most beautiful, sweet, and kind person I've ever known. She can't truly be described. The other truth is I will never not be sad without her here. When I think of her, and that is nonstop, I smile at our memories. I sometimes literally laugh out loud at the many funny ones. At the same time, feeling her physical absence is so very painful. The world is not the same. When sadness wants to take over, I squash my tears just like she always had to. Letting it roll down my face would give it too much power. Tissue is too movie-style romantic. A soft white cloth cannot wipe the pain away and make it all well again. So I squash it with the back of my hand as if it were a bead of sweat on my forehead. It works for a while. Back to how wonderful Nikky was and is. I again feel more lucky to have been her mom than I am sad about my loss.

In the beginning, it was hard to even breathe. I forced myself to look at the stars every night, just for a few seconds. I then gave myself credit for having done so. I spoke to her when I looked at the stars. Any time I smiled or laughed I told myself out loud, "You just smiled. You just laughed." I gave myself credit for being able to do so.

It took kind of a self-training to do this, but when I saw things like Christmas lights, I wanted them to bring back the happy years and not the sadness of what I no longer have. After losing her, I made sure that on every holiday, every anniversary date, I did really happy things. When she was little, Nikky loved 'The Never Ending Story.' But we had to fast forward one part. That was when the horse drowned in the sea of sadness. I refused to sink into that sea. I did the opposite on special days. For example, at Christmas, I threw 'Ugly sweater on steroids' parties. Light-up clothing was encouraged. I spent hours decorating every inch of my tree, creating lovely scenes on each branch. I decked the halls of my entire house from corner to corner. I lit up my entire yard with spiral trees, candy canes, and snowmen. I played all of the music and shared many cups of cheer with friends. My friends seemed to understand and came in their craziest Christmas clothes. I dressed as a Christmas elf. It really worked. You can't be sad when you're surrounded by friends wearing such clothing. It took about three years of kind of forcing myself to do these things on special days before my brain could easily just see things like Christmas lights and be happy. It was kind of a self-hypnosis. I feel if you sink on the first Christmas or anniversary, you will again every single year after. I wasn't willing to be scared as holidays rolled around of how I'd feel, so I took control. It is different for everyone, but this is what worked for me.

I remember the wonderful things about her every single day. I revel in that. I allow the good memories to consume me and stay a part of me.

My love for Nikky and hers for me is not tragic. The loss is. I feel so blessed that I am connected with her forever. This life is but a tiny fleck compared to eternity. Every day, I pray. In those prayers, I always tell God... Thank you, Lord, for allowing me to be Nikky's Mom.

~*~

EPILOGUE
A VISIT FROM NIKKY

Nikky visited me this morning. She communicates every single day, but a visit is different. It's usually when I start to wake up in the morning. This was as well. She came into the room saying, "Mom." So loud and clear. I was in and out of sleep. This was a dream but so real. "Nikky! I yelled with joy! Thank you for visiting me! We were hugging, but she seemed confused. As I pulled back from the hug to look at her, I noticed her long blond hair and her young face. "Nikky, your hair is blond," I said. "How old are you?" "I'm eleven." She said again, confused. I said, "Oh, Nikky, you don't know what happened, do you? You died when you were 21." Her eyes got wide, and then she stared at me with understanding and sadness. Her eyes filled with tears. "Oh." Then she hugged me so much harder. "It's OK, Nikky," I said. Thank you so much for your visits.

Sometimes, she has told me things that would happen that day. Things I had no way of knowing. Very specific things that I had no control over, and they always happened exactly as she said they would. It was like she wanted to prove she was real.

She reached out to me through nature over and over. I often went to Northway Fields to visit her. That is where the police found her. It was Nikky's consideration of me that is the reason she was found there by police and not found by me. We have a history in the Northway Fields. The

Nikky's Note

beginning of the path is at the back of a parking lot. You go from Greenbelt onto this long dirt path through to the woods. It feels like going camping in the mountains. No pavement but dirt and rocks and trees. When you get to the end of the path, it suddenly opens up into the huge fields and two dirt parking lots. You are suddenly greeted by vast sky views and wide open spaces. It feels like you are far away from a city, yet the BW Parkway is just beyond a row of trees. The night view of the sky is magnificent. It's no wonder Greenbelt put an observatory for the stars there. Greenbelters go there with telescopes to have "Star Parties," where they view the sky and things like meteor showers.

Nikky and I went several nights just to sit and look at the stars there. It is a peaceful place. She also played baseball there. Every time I go to see her there, she reaches out. The first winter day after losing her, I brought Kairi there to visit her. It had recently snowed. I kept wondering where exactly her car had been found, but I didn't want to bother the police to ask. Kairi and I got out so she could run around in the snow. There was a car in the corner of the parking lot. We were between the car and the path to get back out. Not knowing when the car would leave, I was being careful with Kairi. She ran around inside the fence but stayed close to the parking lot. When we were ready to leave, I put her leash back on and then noticed the other car was gone. It hadn't gone past us, though. I thought, maybe there is a new path that goes out the other side of the fields. Kairi and I walked over, looking for the path. No path, no car, no tracks, no nothing. It disappeared. I decided that was Nikky answering my question about where her car had been found.

One summer night, a friend and I brought Kairi and Oreo to visit Nikky in the fields. Both dogs were running happily around in the baseball field. I had told the friend that something magical and seemingly impossible happens every time I go there. We were ready to leave when suddenly, all at once, all of the trees around the field lit up with lightning bugs. They were so bright - like Christmas lights! They went from the bottom of the trees up to the very top. "Oh my GOODNESS, this is so beautiful!!" I said. "Can you believe this?" I asked the friend. "Have you ever seen anything like it?" "I have to admit I have not." He said. He hadn't been a believer, but he was after that.

Nikky's Note

HER TREE DEDICATION

On Nikky's birthday following the loss, I planted a little crepe myrtle tree in a field in Greenbelt with a plaque dedicating it to her. We had a ceremony with friends and family at the tree. So many people came. Some I didn't know, but they came because we had something in common. They were parents who had also lost a child. The club no one ever wants to join. There to support another member. After my friend's daughter played her guitar and sang a song and we spoke about Nikky, we walked down the hill. My house was again filled with kind, supportive, and loving friends.

When the City landscaper came to get the tree from my yard to plant it, I took a little one of the shoots that grow around the base of Crepe Myrtle trees. I put it into a pot on my porch that had beautiful wave petunias in it. The little thing surprised me by staying alive. It was hot, and wilting, so I took it inside and put it in water. Again, this little thing kept living. Finally, I planted it in a small pot, which I kept on the table in the sliding doorway. It stayed small for years, but it went through the seasons like a tree. It grew leaves in the spring, and the leaves turned red in fall and fell off during winter. One year, I put it outside, and it grew like crazy into a small tree. I looked it up and those sprouts can't bloom. You need the root ball for blooms. A couple of years later, I put it in an even bigger pot. Sure enough, that little tree started blooming and blooming. It still does. I feel it's yet another way my daughter speaks to me through nature.

When you want to connect with someone you've lost, go outside and watch for the signs.

www.ingramcontent.com/pod-product-compliance
Lightning Source LLC
Chambersburg PA
CBHW041456010526
44107CB00026B/1281/J